D1147207

ONE WEEK LOAN

Acknowledgements

The following people have all contributed in various ways to the accumulation of research data, the interpretation of findings and the preparation of the report: Corinne Aves, Lynn Crosby, Wendy Dear, Brenda Jones, Patricia Lees, Christina Pantazis, Josephine Parker and Lorraine Tollemache. I would like them to know that their help is remembered and appreciated.

Very special thanks should be given to Professor Emeritus Roy Parker, who acted as consultant to the study, and to my co-researcher Gwen Caesar, who was responsible for most of the child interviews. I would also like to record a general debt of gratitude to Dr Carolyn Davies, Michael Brennan and Julia Ridgway at the Department of Health, to Professor June Thoburn and members of the Research Advisory Group, to Mary James and the other directors and staff of the three voluntary agencies that participated in the research, and to the parents and children who made the study possible.

Note about the author

Dr Morag Owen is a Research Fellow in the School of Cultural and Community Studies at the University of Sussex. During the last ten years she has worked on several research studies concerned with child care and child protection. Her published work includes *Voluntary Care in Difficult Cases*, University of East Anglia, 1991, *Social Justice and Children in Care*, Avebury, 1992, and, with Elaine Farmer, *Child Protection Practice: Private risks and public remedies*, HMSO, London, 1995. She has worked in social work and in teaching and is the mother of two children.

Novices, Old hands and Professionals

A study of adoption
by single people

Morag Owen

British

Agencies

for **A**doption

and **F**ostering

Published by
British Agencies for Adoption & Fostering
(BAAF)
Skyline House
200 Union Street
London SE1 0LX

© Morag Owen 1999

Charity registration 275689

**British Library Cataloguing in Publication
Data**
A catalogue record for this book is available
from the British Library

ISBN 1 873868 68 5

Production management by Shaila Shah,
BAAF

Designed by Andrew Haig & Associates
Cover illustration by Andrew Haig
Typeset by Avon Dataset Ltd, Bidford on Avon
Printed by Russell Press Ltd. (TU),
Nottingham

Contents

1.	Introduction	1

SECTION I   BACKGROUND TO THE STUDY

2.	The legal framework of single-person adoption	3
3.	The research and policy context	9
4.	Origins and design of the study	18

SECTION II   THE APPROACH-ROUTE TO ADOPTION

5.	The single adopters	26
6.	The attitudes of referring agencies	39
7.	Experiences of the approval process	51
8.	Linking and placement patterns	64

SECTION III   AFTER THE PLACEMENT

9.	Post-placement child care	74
10.	Employment and finances	87
11.	Family and community relationships	100
12.	Changes in the family over time	113
13.	Contact with the child's birth family	122

SECTION IV   OUTCOMES AND CONCLUSIONS

14.	The experiences of the children	135
15.	Placement outcomes	169
16.	Implications for policy and practice	180
	References	188

1 Introduction

This book presents findings and conclusions from a research study of single-person adoption, undertaken with funding from the Department of Health (DoH) between 1993 and 1995. The work was based in the School for Policy Studies at Bristol University.

Aims of the research
The research set out to document and comment on the experiences of single adopters and their children. It was concerned with both process and outcome. In other words the topics to be investigated included features of the systems by which the adopters were approved and supported, as well as the experiences of adults and children in the aftermath of the placement. Some estimate was also made of the children's progress.

The timing of the study
The proposal for the research was drawn up shortly after the Government's *Review of Adoption Law* was published as a consultation document in October 1992, and the research itself was started just before the publication of the ensuing White Paper, *Adoption: The future*, in November 1993. It was, and still is, a time of great interest in adoption. The changes described in the White Paper were the first major developments in adoption law and practice for nearly two decades. They were intended to reflect the new understanding of the rights and responsibilities of parents, the duties of public authorities, and the rights of children as enshrined in the Children Act 1989 and the United Nations Convention on the Rights of the Child. Since then there has been publication of a major consultative document, *Adoption – A Service for Children* (DoH and Welsh Office, 1996), which includes the draft of a new Adoption Bill.

Research sample and methodology

The suggestion that a study of single-person adoption should be specifically undertaken came originally from one voluntary adoption agency – the Independent Adoption Service (IAS) in London. The research with IAS adopters produced a great deal of interesting material, and after the first 12 months it was extended to include two other voluntary adoption agencies, namely the Manchester Adoption Society and the Thomas Coram Foundation.

The final research sample was composed of two groups of people. Firstly, there were 30 single adults (28 women and two men), all of whom contacted an adoption agency and made a successful application for a child at some time in the last ten years. Secondly, and most importantly, there were the 48 children who had been placed with them.

In the compilation of the research report material has been drawn from semi-structured interviews with parents and children, from pre-coded schedules and from file studies, in addition to relevant literature. The schedules were those used in the 'Looking After Children' project (Parker *et al*, 1991; Ward, 1995).

The role of the research

In spite of the widespread assumptions that have been made about family status and structure, the relevance of single parenthood in adoption has not been widely studied. This is a deficit which we set out to remedy, at least in part. However, the issues of adoption and single parenting are hedged around by moral and political considerations, for they touch on vitally important matters – not only the relationship which exists or should exist between parents and children, but the relationship between men and women, relatives and non-relatives, people of different ethnic backgrounds or different cultures, professionals and non-professionals, public and private agencies, the family and the state.

The findings and conclusions of this study are intended to contribute to an ongoing debate. In the long run it will be for policy-makers and practitioners, parents and adoptees to decide, on the basis of evidence presented here and elsewhere, how far this unique form of family-building may contribute to the care of vulnerable children in post-millennium Britain.

2 The legal framework of single-person adoption

Ever since the first legislation on adoption in England and Wales in 1926, the law has allowed applications to adopt to be made by single people as well as married couples. However, there has always been a strong presumption that adopters would be selected mainly from the ranks of married couples, who are said to enjoy 'the most common permanent relationship in which the upbringing of children is undertaken' (DoH and Welsh Office, 1993).

The general trend over several decades has been towards increasing professionalisation of adoption practice, and recent debates about adoption law must be seen in that context. As far as the eligibility and suitability of adopters are concerned, the task of the law has always been to set necessary boundaries; but within the legislative framework there is much scope for discretion on the part of adoption agencies. This means that actual decisions about the approval of adopters, both married and single, must take into account not only legal regulations but agency policies and the principles of professional practice.

When these matters are formally discussed, the debate is not usually confined to the content of legal or professional guidelines. It is also about the boundary between the two.

The current legislative framework

The statutory work of adoption agencies in England and Wales is at present defined by the Adoption Act 1976 – a consolidating Act which brought together provisions from the Adoption Act 1958 and the Children Act 1975. In the current legislation married couples and single people applying to adopt are given approximately equal status as far as eligibility is concerned. Both single people and married couples are subject to the same restrictions of domicile and minimum age. This means that a single person (or at least one of a married couple) who wishes to apply for an adoption order must be domiciled in part of the United Kingdom, the Channel Islands or the Isle of Man, and any prospective adopter must also be at least 21 years old.

In addition to the requirements about domicile and minimum age, the 1976 Act contains certain conditions about marital status which affect the range of opportunities for single adopters. Paradoxically, these legal restrictions appear to be aimed primarily at married or cohabiting couples rather than at single people who are living on their own or with relatives. There are concerns about the social and legal status of vanished or cohabiting partners. A married person may only adopt alone if the spouse cannot be found or is incapable of applying by reason of physical or mental ill-health – or if the members of the couple have separated and are living apart and if the separation is likely to be permanent.

The present legislation prohibits unmarried couples from adopting jointly, and neither the Review of Adoption Law nor the ensuing White Paper nor the Draft Adoption Bill has suggested that this should be changed, not least because that prohibition was specified in Article 6(1) of the European Adoption Convention. Couples who are cohabiting in a steady relationship cannot therefore apply jointly to adopt a child, and the only solution in these circumstances is for one member of the couple to apply as a single person.

In our research study we did not interview single adopters who were cohabiting, since from a social point of view they might be considered to have a *de facto* marriage. From a legal point of view, however, their position is somewhat problematic. It is interesting to note that the law apparently has fewer problems in defining the eligibility of applicants who are totally single in the sense that they have no resident partner.

The impact of the Review of Adoption Law

Adoption was not included in the review of child care law which was carried out prior to the Children Act 1989. Instead, a separate review of adoption law was initiated in 1989. Extensive consultation was followed by four discussion papers and a review report, which led in 1993 to the publication of the government White Paper, *Adoption: The future*.

In its discussion of family structure, the Review of Adoption Law (1992) lent support to adoption in the context of legal marriage. In so doing it put forward a number of arguments to support the ban on joint application by unmarried couples. Since unmarried parents do not have the same legal obligations to one another as people who are married, it was suggested that the caring parent might be less financially secure if the relationship were to break down. It was also suggested that other family members might be less willing to accept the adopted child as part of their family if the parents were not married. As the BAAF response to the Review (1993) pointed out, some of these social arguments are unconvincing. There is little reason to suppose that cohabiting couples in a stable relationship will offer less security to a child because they are not married, or that their families will behave differently towards the adopted child for this reason. Furthermore the existing regulations ensure that each member of a cohabiting couple will be assessed before the placement is undertaken, in the expectation that each person will have a parental role.

There are, however, some cogent legal arguments against joint approval of cohabiting couples. Firstly, it is considered important for adoption practice in the United Kingdom to match the conditions of the European Adoption Convention, to ensure consistency of standards. Secondly, there is a strong underlying argument that two people who are entering into a legal relationship with a child should also have a legal relationship with each other. In this as in other respects, the practices of law and social work do not always coincide.

From the point of view of our study, the very existence of so much controversy highlights the fact that single-person adoption is considered a second-best option for cohabiting couples, or for married people whose relationship has clearly failed. In the process of this discussion, the position of totally single people has not been enhanced. This point was articulated in the *BAAF Response to the Review of Adoption Law* (1993), as follows:

> *The unhelpful emphasis placed on the importance of adopters' married status can do serious harm to the interests of a number of children. Single adopters continue to offer a very specific and immensely valuable resource in placing particular children for whom adoption with one adult, in preference to two, best meets the child's needs.*

The arguments of the *Review of Adoption Law* and its accompanying responses were picked up and developed in the ensuing White Paper, *Adoption: The future*. It is clearly anticipated in this document that some applications for single-person adoption will come from people who have *de facto* marriages. However, the White Paper recognises that 'some children, often with special needs, are successfully adopted by unmarried women, women no longer married or women widowed early'. The statement about single people continues, cautiously:

> *The devotion and care they can bring to children often rightly commands admiration. There may, too, be a small number of other exceptional circumstances where adoption by a single person may be sensible – for example a widowed step-father with whom the child has already lived before the mother's death.*

In short, single-person adoption is given a regular role, but a severely limited role, in a spectrum of arrangements for substitute child care. The rest of the White Paper continues to endorse the general preference for adoption by married couples, and it ends the section dealing with family structure by recommending 'particularly careful matching' in cases where this is not judged to be the best option.

Recent proposals for new legislation
Like the Acts which preceded it, the Draft Adoption Bill has remained relatively silent on the precise criteria for selecting adopters, since this task is regarded as falling within the discretion of adoption agencies rather than being a matter for legislation. The Bill repeats the existing ban on joint adoption by unmarried couples; but in Clause 45(1) it reaffirms the right of a single person to apply. It says, simply:

> *An adoption order may be made on the application of one person who has attained the age of 21 years and is not married.*

No upper age limit is suggested, although the possibility of introducing one had been given careful consideration at the review stage. Consequently, if this Bill becomes law, it will still be possible for single women or men to adopt when they are beyond the usual child-bearing age. (This may be of benefit to some older children.) The position of applicants from minority ethnic groups may also be enhanced by the fact that the provisions for domicile have been extended, to take account of the fact that some people who wish to adopt may have lived in this country for some time but retain a domicile overseas. The right to apply is now no longer confined to people who are domiciled in the British Isles, since one year's habitual residence can be an alternative basis of jurisdiction [Clause 43(2) and 43(3)].

On a more general level, the proposals of the Draft Adoption Bill bring adoption policy into line with the Children Act by making the child's welfare paramount in decision-making. The proposed Clause 1(2) of the Draft Bill, which has been widely welcomed by agencies such as BAAF (Cullen, 1996), says:

> *The paramount consideration of the court or adoption agency must be the child's welfare, in childhood and later.*

In other words adoption is confirmed as a service for children rather than for adults. Furthermore, in their interpretation of 'the child's welfare' both courts and adoption agencies need to take an extremely long-term view.

It seems likely that this amendment to existing legislation will eventually reach the statute books. Whether or not this happens quickly, however, the paramountcy of the child's welfare is now an important principle underlying much of our child care legislation, and it is against this criterion that adoption by single people must be judged.

Summary

- The statutory work of adoption agencies in England and Wales is currently defined by the Adoption Act 1976. Single people have been allowed to adopt since the first legislation in 1926, but married couples have always been the preferred choice of adoption agencies.
- The main legal restrictions are concerned with domicile and minimum age. Prospective single adopters must be domiciled in part of the United Kingdom, the Channel Islands or the Isle of Man, and they must be at least 21 years old.
- The legislation also contains conditions about marital status. A married person may only adopt alone if the spouse cannot be found

or is incapable of applying – or if the members of the couple have separated and the separation is likely to be permanent. Unmarried couples cannot adopt jointly.

- The impression created by some of the discussion surrounding the legislation is that single-person adoption is a second-best option for cohabiting couples. This is unfair because it obscures the contribution made by totally single people, who are the subject of this research.

- The White Paper, *Adoption: The future*, which was published in 1993 following the Government's *Review of Adoption Law*, recognises that 'some children, often with special needs, are successfully adopted by unmarried women, women no longer married or women widowed early'. However, it recommends particularly careful matching in these cases.

- The proposals of the Draft Adoption Bill published in 1996, if carried through into legislation, will bring adoption policy into line with the Children Act 1989 by ensuring that 'the paramount consideration of the court or adoption agency must be the child's welfare'. Good practice already dictates that both single applicants and married couples should be assessed according to this criterion.

3 The research and policy context

In an early edition of her guide for adoptive parents, Jane Rowe said that 'it seems foolish to take a child from one single woman and give him to another' (Rowe, 1969). In the climate of the 1950s and 1960s, this statement was probably not out of place. It assumed, first of all, that most of the parents giving up children for adoption were single mothers with illegitimate babies who needed a father; secondly, that a transfer from one single woman to another would produce no improvement (which suggests strongly that family status was considered to be the main factor determining children's welfare); and thirdly, that single mothers could be identified as a homogeneous group, irrespective of whether they were divorced, widowed or never-married.

In the last 30 years it is clear that the situation has moved on. The characteristics of people wishing to adopt and the population of children available for adoption have changed. In more recent editions of her book, Rowe admits that an increasing number of agencies will now consider applications from a single man or woman to adopt a child who is older, physically disabled or with special emotional needs. She even suggests that some severely disabled children 'can benefit from the intensity of devotion that perhaps only a single parent can give' (Rowe, 1982). At the same time attitudes to unusual family structures in the community have become modified, and the number of children requiring adoption placements has increased. This has opened the way for greater consideration of non-traditional families in adoption (Caine, 1990).

Research on adoption and family status
Although the experiences of single adoptive parents in this country are still largely unknown, there is a useful body of research on single adoptive parenting in the USA, much of it conducted by way of small studies during the 1960s and 1970s. Many of the findings are positive. For example, Jordan and Little (1966) found that single adoptive mothers

possessed an 'above-average child orientation' and developed healthy mother–child relationships. Branham (1970) also found that children and parents had formed healthy relationships, and recommended single-parent families as a resource for special needs children. This judgement did not imply that single women should be treated as second-class adopters, but that many of them possessed higher than average skills.

In a large-scale survey conducted in the 1970s, Feigelman and Silverman (1977) compared children adopted by couples and by single people. No significant differences were found in the children's physical or emotional health or social development; but single parents whose friends and relatives responded positively to the adoptions were much more likely to judge that their adopted child had made an excellent adjustment. Six years after the initial study, the adjustment of children raised by single-parent adopters remained similar to that of children raised by adoptive couples. Another survey by Dougherty (1978) reported that single adoptive mothers were personally mature, had viable social support systems, and were aware of their own needs as well as those of their children. Dougherty's conclusions, like those of previous researchers, were decidedly supportive of placements with adoptive single parents.

The studies by Dougherty, and by Feigelman and Silverman, can of course be criticised on the grounds that information was obtained initially from postal surveys, which may have failed to represent the population of single adoptive parents (although all the surveys had a good response rate). The most useful empirical research so far is probably that done by Shireman and Johnson (1976 and 1985), who conducted a longitudinal study of single adoptive parenting during the 1970s and 1980s. Their initial sample included 31 black single parents who had adopted children younger than three years old. When the children were four years old, the researchers noted concerns about the extreme isolation of some parents and the intense relationships between parents and children; but the isolation of the single parents is said to have been lessened when the children entered school. When Shireman (1988) interviewed some of the same children in adolescence, no significant differences in adjustment were observed among adopted and non-adopted children, or among those who had experienced single-parent, two-parent or transracial adoptions. The intensity of relationship noted by Shireman has since been recognised as a positive feature, where single-parent adopters are successfully matched with extremely deprived children, and some recent studies of placement outcomes have also emphasised the importance of commitment and a willingness to persevere (Borland *et al*, 1991).

Has the research on disruption anything to tell us about the importance of family status? Since single parents are equally represented in disrupted and in intact adoptions (Barth and Berry, 1988), it seems that marital status has little if any effect on disruption. Social support is reported to be a much better predictor of stability. In Barth and Berry's study the adoptive parents received social support in a number of different ways, which included having relatives in the area, having friends who were foster or adoptive parents, and being affiliated to a church or other organisation. The interacting characteristics of parent and child, irrespective of family status, were clearly important as a means of enabling the child to perform developmental tasks. Groze and Rosenthal actually found that there were *fewer problems* among children in single-parent adoptive families, when compared with traditional two-parent adoptions, and that single parents were more likely to evaluate the adoption as very positive. They concluded that 'flexibility is critically important in the assessment process' and that adoption policies should deliberately target non-traditional families in recruitment (Groze and Rosenthal, 1991).

When the group of single-parent adopters is extended to single parents in general, there is more British research available. Once again, however, the stereotype needs to be questioned. Many of the child-rearing difficulties associated with single parenthood seem to be off-shoots of poverty and deprivation (Kumar, 1993; Bradshaw and Millar, 1994; Middleton *et al*, 1995). Others may be connected with the experience of family disruption, which frequently includes domestic violence as well as separation and divorce, and which has resulted in some vulnerable mothers and children being forced to live on their own after undergoing traumatic experiences (Hague and Malos, 1993; Burghes, 1994; Hester *et al*, 1994).

One stereotype of the "lone parent" is the young, teenage mother who accidentally becomes pregnant and is obliged to remain unwillingly dependent on her parents or to live alone in poor circumstances. It would be surprising if single adoptive parents, who are approved on grounds of experience and who parent by choice, conformed to this negative image. The incidence of the stereotype itself fluctuates, and if a long-term view is taken it may seem to be declining. According to research at the Family Policy Studies Centre (Burghes and Brown, 1995), there were 10,000 fewer teenage maternities in 1991 than 1981, and more than 40,000 fewer than in 1971. At the same time there has been a decline in "shotgun marriages" and a rise in stable cohabitation. In all the available accounts there is an element of positive or negative social construction, depending on whether single-parent families are viewed from what Green and Crooks call the 'structural deficit perspective', which focuses on pathology, or the 'structurally adaptive perspective' which takes into account the families' strengths and resilience (Green and Crooks, 1988).

Do the children of single parents present special difficulties in adolescence? Adolescence can trigger problems for all children, and those in single-parent families are no exception. Dornbusch *et al* (1985) examined patterns of family decision-making and found that there was some reduction in the control of adolescents in mother-only families, resulting in a greater incidence of deviance, but they also claimed that:

> *The presence of any other adult in a mother-only household brings control levels closer to those found in two-parent families. This suggests that there are functional equivalents of two-parent families – non-traditional groupings that can do the job of parenting.*

Another point about family structure which is often forgotten, but which has been emphasised in some recent studies of both adoptive and non-adoptive families, is that the child's experience is strongly affected by sibling groupings (Dunn, 1984; Rushton *et al*, 1989; Wedge and Mantle, 1991; Kosonen, 1994). The peer group also has a positive part to play in introducing the child to cultural meanings, and making him or her feel part of a recognisable social world (Richards and Light, 1986). Both family and community structure are more complex, and probably more influential, than a simple focus on the parent–child relationship allows.

The notion of equivalence

Various writers have pointed out that in order to protect the interests of both children and parents, the adoptive family has traditionally been made to resemble the two-parent "natural family" as closely as possible (Kirk and McDaniel, 1984). The reasoning is that any deviation from this pattern may be considered disadvantageous – partly because the two-parent family lifestyle is considered not only normal but optimal as a framework for the upbringing of children, and partly because the adopted child in an unconventional family setting is often considered to be more vulnerable. When children are already vulnerable by reason of past experiences, it can justifiably be claimed that we have an extra duty not to put obstacles in their way.

Clearly we need to seek the views of single adopters and their children to see what effect the various images of normality have had, firstly on the parents' motivation to adopt and secondly on the family's experience of the adoption. In the pluralist communities of Britain in the 1990s, we can also ask how far the presumed norm can be seen to exist. In fact it may never have existed, even as a statistical reality. For some writers the important point is that it exists as an ideal, which has to be striven for if the family is to be helped to fulfil its function of 'linking autonomous individuals to the macrostructure of modern society' (Berger, 1993). In Berger's words:

> This type of family, more than any other, is peculiarly suited for producing self-reliant, morally accountable and entrepreneurial individuals who become the carriers of political responsibility and economic prosperity.

The evidence on which this statement is based is uncertain; but the perceived need to shore up the nuclear family can exercise a powerful influence on the general direction of family policy. It has been suggested by Kirk and McDaniel (1984) that adoption policies in the USA, and perhaps to a lesser extent in Britain, have tried to embody certain idealised images of the mainstream family and to prop up this idealisation. The model of family life which has traditionally been used in the adoption approval process may not actually resemble very closely those that are in current usage. At the same time the temptation to use

13

adoption as a "marker" or standard-setter for the rest of society must be strong, in a situation where people are campaigning for social change. Adoptive families are artificially constructed, and this is one form of family life over which the state agencies have an unprecedented degree of control.

There is, however, a deeper notion of equivalence. Along with concerns about the "normality" of certain family structures there is a feeling that the adoptive family must reproduce a model of family life based on consanguinity. Adoption is concerned with social rather than biological parenting, and if single adopters achieve parity with adoptive couples in some respects, both groups may still feel "different" when compared with those who have their own birth children.

The acknowledgement of difference
Contemporary adoption practice encourages parents to recognise that adoption is at least partly an artificial process, which does not mimic the two-parent birth family but replaces it with something that is similar but different. One possible implication of this policy is that alternative family structures are worthy of being treated with greater flexibility.

Public acceptance of the "difference" of the adopted child was boosted in 1975 by the provisions for children to contact birth parents after the age of 18. These provisions implied that the identity of the child could never be totally swamped by his or her adoptive family, regardless of its composition. At the same time more credence is currently being given to the idea of mixed or dual identity – a notion that has been found to appeal strongly to some children of mixed parentage (Tizard and Phoenix, 1993). Contact with the child's birth family, either direct or indirect, is increasingly seen as being in the child's best interests. A major objection to unusual adoptions is removed if it can be shown that the child's sense of identity is not necessarily confused or undermined by these arrangements.

Again, we need to know the views of adoptive parents and children on these issues. Several writers have warned against applying Kirk's "acknowledgement of difference" doctrine too enthusiastically. Carole Smith, for example, points out that Kirk did not demonstrate an empirical relationship between the acknowledgement of difference and successful outcome in terms of a happier, more satisfying or qualitatively better environment for adopted children. He merely hypothesised that this relationship existed (Smith, 1984). There are other researchers, such as McWhinnie in 1967, Triseliotis in 1973 and Raynor in 1980, who have emphasised the adopted child's need for security and a sense of belonging, and who have claimed that a preoccupation with difference may too easily destroy these vital ingredients.

In short, we need to investigate the ways in which these single parents and their children feel similar to or different from others, and the impact which these factors have on the adoption. It may be helpful to ask whether the single adopters see themselves primarily as single parents, or as adoptive parents, or simply as mothers and fathers. However, other descriptions may be relevant. If the parents feel that they are in any way unusual, it may not be because they are single adopters but because they have adopted older children with special needs, or because they seem to have been chosen for a highly specialised task.

The importance of the family life-cycle

In its early stages the adoption process is firmly rooted in social work practice but it does not totally belong there. A perspective based on the family life-cycle unites some elements of equivalence with the acknowledgement of difference. Basically it suggests that although the adoptive family is artificially created, in the actual experience of living together both the single adopter and her child are involved in a developmental journey which is similar in many ways to that experienced by other families in the community.

Helpful literature puts this journey into a wider historical context – the trend towards older motherhood as well as more frequent cohabitation, the continuing growth of single parenthood (death of a partner being replaced by divorce as a reason for singleness), and the effect of increasing independence in the elderly (Anderson, 1980 and 1990). The relationship between marriage patterns, income and employment is particularly significant, since it affects the lifestyle of the family and consequently the experiences of children within it (Lewis, 1993; Land, 1994). Many single women adopters have no need to turn to marriage for financial security and – if married – may well end up supporting their partners.

It is helpful to see the development of attitudes towards marriage in general as moving from the institutional to the relational, and to bear in mind that many women who seek to adopt may have escaped from marriages that were simply institutional. It is a considerable achievement if they have managed difficult transitions in their own lives, and if they can help adopted children to do the same.

As well as the historical material, there is some recent literature on partner relationships and parenthood. Particularly interesting is the idea that marriage and parenthood can be conceived as two distinct institutions (Clulow and Mattinson, 1989; Cowan and Cowan, 1992) and that parenthood has often worked to reassert the traditional divisions between the sexes. Some single adopters in the study may possibly share these views. It is also interesting to know that studies have been made of the transition to parenthood and its impact on partnerships, and that in many cases the transition is by no means easy (Michaels and Goldberg, 1988). We need to be reminded that marriage is not a single entity but a series of hurdles, some of which can be surmounted more easily than others, and that the interests involved in maintaining the partnership may not necessarily be congruent with those of the child.

In a context such as this, the paramountcy of the child's welfare in adoption starts to take on a new meaning. Recruitment processes cannot afford to concentrate too heavily on family structure and status, without taking into consideration the quality of relationships and the likely experience of the child. Furthermore, the notion of permanency does not imply that family relationships are fossilised at the point when the order is made, since both before and after the adoption, single carers are engaged in a developmental journey which is undertaken by two-parent adopters and by parents in birth families as well.

In all these situations, the child's welfare must depend on how far the parents – whether single or married, natural or adoptive – are willing and able to perform their tasks.

Summary

- Since the 1950s and 1960s, the population of children available for adoption has changed. As the supply of illegitimate babies has declined, older children have increased as a proportion of all children adopted. Many of them have special needs.

- Most of the available research on adoption by single people was carried out in the USA during the 1970s and 1980s. The findings are generally positive. The adopters were found to be highly committed and personally mature, and to have viable social support systems.

- Whether or not the two-parent family is "the norm", it still acts as a standard-setter. Adoptive families are artificially constructed and this is one form of family life over which the state has an unprecedented degree of control.

- Public acknowledgement of the "difference" of adoptive families has been boosted by the provisions for adopted children to contact birth parents at the age of 18, and by increased contact between the adoptive family and the child's birth family at an earlier stage. These developments, together with changes in the population of children for adoption, may make it easier for single adopters to find acceptance.

- The permanent linking of single people and children can be seen in the context of the family life-cycle. The transition to parenthood is one of a series of transitions which the prospective adopters have to make, in company with all other parents whether married or single.

4 Origins and design of the study

The idea that a study of single-person adoption should be specifically undertaken came originally from one voluntary adoption agency – the Independent Adoption Service (IAS) in London. This small, multiracial and non-sectarian agency specialises in finding families for children referred by the local authorities. At the start of the ten-year period from 1984 to 1994, the agency had successfully recruited a number of black British adopters of African and African-Caribbean origins, some of whom were single women. Most of them had been widowed or divorced. In the late 1980s and early 1990s these black adopters were joined by an increasing number of white single people, and more of the applicants who were approved for adoption had never been married.

It should be noted that the total number of single people approved for adoption is still small. The record of approvals by the IAS adoption panel for the five-year period 1989–94 shows that 17 single applicants were accepted, although the number of couples selected during the same period was 134. Even in an agency which was sympathetic to single applicants, therefore, the majority of the work was with couples, and in terms of successful approvals the single people accounted for only 11 per cent of the total. This figure is roughly in accord with the findings of another large-scale quantitative study of adoption patterns, which recently reported that only six per cent of the adopters approved by local authorities and nine per cent of those approved by voluntary adoption agencies were single (Dance, 1997).

At the time of our research some of the single adoptive parents were still known to IAS, either because they attended social gatherings such as the annual picnic or because they were in the process of adopting other children. Not all of the adopters were in touch with the agency, however, and the social workers who had helped them felt that it would be beneficial to know of their experiences. It was also realised that there was a dearth of research material on single-person adoption, with the exception of the older American studies mentioned in Chapter 3. After the first 12 months the study was extended to include two other agencies which had approved a number of single adopters – namely the Manchester Adoption Society and the Thomas Coram Foundation.

Research sample and methodology

During the course of the research a number of adoptive applicants were interviewed, including three single women who had wanted to adopt but who had withdrawn at various points during the approval process. The main research sample, however, was composed of two groups of people. Firstly there were 30 single adults (28 women and two men), all of whom had contacted an adoption agency and made a successful application for a child at some time in the last ten years. Secondly, and most importantly, there were the 48 children who had been placed with them.

As previously mentioned, none of the single people in the study were in a cohabiting relationship at the time of the application, since the research design excluded those applicants who might be considered to have a *de facto* marriage. When the placement was made, the single adopters in the study were living alone or with relatives and none had a resident partner.

A series of three interviews was planned for each adoptive household: the first with the parent, the second with the child, and the third with parent and child together. The first two interviews, which were often carried out simultaneously by the researchers in separate rooms, were tape-recorded. Their main purpose was to enable parents and children to talk about their experiences both before and after the adoption. The third interview was not tape-recorded. Instead, the aim was to collect the specific information needed for the "Looking After Children Schedules" – standardised questionnaires on child care outcomes which were to be completed during the interview.

The fourth and final part of the research consisted of a study of agency files.

First data source: the interviews with adoptive parents

At the start of the study introductory letters were sent to all the single applicants for whom we had been given names and addresses. The actual situation of the adopters or prospective adopters varied, since the original list of single applicants who had contacted the IAS included some who had withdrawn in addition to the people who had actually had children placed with them. The legal status of the placed children also varied, since in some cases the adoption had not yet been completed.

Our introductory letters and those from the agency were followed up by telephone calls to make personal contact and arrange visits. In the course of these arrangements we were anxious not to be too closely identified with the adoption agency; but in general the parents seemed to understand quite accurately the nature of the research task, and only three people who had previously been approved by IAS refused to take part in the study. Unfortunately seven more parents could not be reached because they had moved house, or because their telephone lines were "empty", or because they had ex-directory telephone numbers with a ban on calls transmitted by way of the operator. To increase the size of the sample, and also to make it less likely that children with distinctive case histories could be traced through our report, the Manchester Adoption Society and the Thomas Coram Foundation were invited to join the study in August 1994. The number and percentage of children entering the sample from each adoption agency is given in Table 1.

Table 1

The adoption agencies

Agency	No. of children in the sample	Per cent
Independent Adoption Service	24	50
Thomas Coram Foundation	13	27
Manchester Adoption Society	11	23
Totals	48	100

Table 2
The children in the sample, grouped according to age, sex and ethnicity

Age	No. of white children		No. of black children		Total no. of children in the sample
	M	F	M	F	
1	–	–	–	–	–
2	–	–	–	1	1
3	–	–	1	2	3
4	1	–	2	–	3
5	1	–	1	–	2
6	–	1	3	1	5
7	–	3	–	–	3
8	–	–	1	–	1
9	1	–	1	1	3
10	4	2	–	1	7
11	2	1	–	–	3
12	2	1	1	–	4
13	–	4	–	–	4
14	1	1	–	–	2
15	2	1	–	–	3
16	2	–	–	–	2
17	–	1	1	–	2
Totals	16	15	11	6	48

Second data source: the interviews with children

The planning of the initial child interviews had to be done with special care, since we were anxious to avoid putting undue pressure on the children. We agreed that they would be interviewed only if they were six years old or over, if their parents gave consent and if they were willing to take part.

To preserve consistency as much as possible, the role of child-interviewer was separated from the role of parent-interviewer. All the interviews with children in the IAS sample were carried out by a black researcher, while a white researcher was responsible for the parent interviews. In effect this meant that most families – with the exception of those who refused or whose children were very young – were visited by a black worker and a white worker and had the opportunity to talk to both people.

We agreed that no distinction would be made according to the ethnicity of the children, and the emphasis in planning the research was on good interviewing skills. Nevertheless, the fact that a sympathetic black person was talking to them may have helped some of the black and minority ethnic children to feel more confident. (The sample included 10 children who were of African or African-Caribbean origin and seven who were of mixed parentage.) The interview schedule was varied as much as was necessary to make the children feel at ease, and extensive use was made of drawing materials so that even young or inarticulate children could explain how they saw their families.

Out of the 48 children in the study (see Table 2), 21 have been interviewed. Of those who were not interviewed, nine were too young, that is, under the age of six. Another nine had Down's Syndrome and it was felt by their adoptive parents that they would simply be confused by the questions. Other researchers have found this judgement to be justified (Mason *et al*, 1998). However, 12 children had mild to moderate learning difficulties and most of them were interviewed.

The interviewees were reasonably representative of the whole group in terms of gender and ethnicity. Encouragingly, there were only three parents who did not give permission for their children to be interviewed in cases where the children were old enough and were not mentally disabled. Six children were excluded in this way, and in one of these cases the refusal was said to have come from a child who wished to protect her own privacy. The other three children who were not interviewed were excluded for purely practical reasons, such as the child not being available at the time when visits were planned.

Young children were willing to use pens, pencils, crayons and paper to portray their families, either pictorially or in symbolic form. The purpose of this exercise was communication, but it was also at least partly play. We hoped that play would provide the children with a way of thinking over difficult experiences and keeping or restoring a sense of mastery which might be transferred to other activities (Erikson, 1968; Case and Dalley, 1990; Cattanach, 1992). We were aware that the issues and feelings raised could lead to a need for further discussion, however, and it was reassuring to know that the adoptive parents were willing to see that these needs were met.

The children needed a gentle approach and constant reassurance; but their ready response to the interview, and their appreciation of our wish to know about the people who were important to them, suggest that they used both words and pictures in an attempt to help us to understand their family relationships. At a later stage, our interpretation of the pictures was aided by two consultants at the Tavistock Clinic.

Third data source: the "Looking After Children" schedules

Many people working in the field of child welfare will be familiar with the Looking After Children project. It began as a Department of Health working party which set out to consider the concept of outcome in child care, as an aid to developing a practicable scheme for assessing children's progress (Parker *et al*, 1991; Ward, 1995). Starting from a notion of "reasonable parenting" the working party identified seven developmental dimensions along which children need to progress if they are to achieve satisfactory long-term outcomes. The seven dimensions, which underlie the questions in all the main schedules, are as follows:

1. Health;
2. Education;
3. Identity;
4. Family and social relationships;
5. Social presentation;
6. Emotional and behavioural development;
7. Self-care skills.

The Looking After Children project provided two types of schedule which were used in our research. The first was a questionnaire known as the Basic Facts Sheet, which recorded essential information about the child and family. The second was a more detailed questionnaire known as the Assessment and Action Record. This last schedule was useful as an aid to charting the "outcome" of the adoptions within different age groups, developmentally defined. The age groups and numbers of children in each are given in Table 3.

The original schedules were of course designed as practice tools rather than research instruments and their application to research is still

Table 3
Age groups used in the 'Looking After Children' schedules

Age group	Frequency	Per cent
1–2	1	2
3–4	6	13
5–9	14	29
10–15	23	48
16+	4	8
Totals	48	100

being developed (Ward, 1995). In their existing form they were not ideally suited to adoption research and they had to be adapted, for example, by recording details of contact with the child's birth family separately from interactions within the adoptive family. More importantly, we had to be cautious in our use of the schedule material because of the danger of discriminating against children with long-term disabilities, or extrapolating unfairly from information which ideally should have formed part of a series of recordings rather than being gathered in a research interview which was a "one-off" event.

In spite of these disadvantages, the collection of the schedule material provided a valuable focus for the final interview, and it also generated important information about the outcome of the adoptions at the point when our interviews were conducted. Material relating to the main dimensions was discussed in detail with the parents, and also with older children who chose to participate. This enabled us to have a much fuller record of progress in those key areas of the children's experience.

Fourth data source: the file study
With the permission of the adoptive parents and where necessary with the permission of the children, we carried out a brief study of the records held by the adoption agencies. The main purpose of this study was to fill in some of the gaps in our knowledge of the children's

backgrounds, since adoptive parents and children could not be expected to know or remember all the details of previous placements.

The agency files contained much helpful material in the form of official documents – not simply the "Schedule 2 Report" which had been prepared for the court at the time of the adoption and which contained the social worker's assessment, but also referral forms and associated correspondence, the BAAF forms "E" and "F" (which gave early descriptions of children's estimated needs and the prospective parents' resources), the reports of planning meetings or inter-agency agreements, and in some cases placement record sheets and post-placement reviews. The resulting data proved to be somewhat incomplete, since the records were up to ten years old. However, the material that we were able to collect was valuable.

In the final analysis the different strands of data were brought together in order to produce a picture of each adoption on a case-by-case basis, before attempts were made to identify patterns in the total study.

Summary

- The present research was set up to document and comment on the experiences of single adopters and their children, and to make some estimate of the children's progress.
- The starting point for the research shows that single-person adoption is still fairly rare. The study was initiated by an adoption agency that was sympathetic to single applicants; yet single people accounted for only 11 per cent of approvals over a five-year period.
- In all, three voluntary adoption agencies were involved in bringing forward families for the research. The research sample consisted of 30 single adults and 48 children.
- The data collection was planned in four parts – a semi-structured interview with the adopters and another with children over the age of six, then a third interview to complete the questionnaires known as "Looking After Children" schedules. The fourth part was a study of records.
- Wherever possible, children over the age of six were interviewed in private. They were encouraged to portray their families in drawings and sketches. A total of 21 children were interviewed in this way.

5 The single adopters

Although the single adopters in the study formed a heterogeneous group with widely varied backgrounds, interests and experiences, it was clear from the interviews that they had certain qualities in common. The first was commitment. The belief that they had the capacity to form a relationship with a child – in spite of age or infertility or the lack of a partner – fuelled their determination to adopt.

> *I would have liked to have had a child but for some reason it never happened. I thought I would be a good mother.*

> *I've never been a parent. I don't know anything about children . . . But I felt that when I open my front door and child X comes through the door, we would deal with things together as they came along.*

> *It's this feeling of wanting to share and give a child a chance.*

Interestingly enough, the people who withdrew or were rejected remained committed to the notion of single-person adoption. The statements quoted above were not made by successful applicants; they are taken from interviews with people who failed to complete the process. One of these women had fallen out with the adoption agency and decided to postpone her application to another time and place, while the second was taking time to work through her feelings about children and partners. The third was forced to suspend her application against her will because of a serious and possibly life-threatening illness.

Parenthood was essential to the adopters' sense of identity (Goffman, 1963; Ungerson, 1990). People who failed to complete the process, even though they understood and accepted the outcome, felt that their family structure was incomplete, whereas most of the applicants who had children placed with them, whether or not the adoption had been legally finalised, described their immediate family as consisting of themselves and the placed child or children. In their eyes the nuclear family was *created* at the point when the child was placed for adoption.

Two-parent adoptions and normal births can be seen as heralding the transition to family status in a similar way, since parenthood holds a central place in defining a family (Daly, 1992). For single applicants the transition may have seemed particularly eventful because there was no "nuclear couple". This does not, however, imply that the children adopted by the single people were isolated either in terms of relationships or in living arrangements, as a study of their circumstances shows.

Household composition

Tables 4 and 5 show the composition of the households in which children were living after having been adopted or placed for adoption with a single person. In 27 per cent of cases one adult (the parent or prospective parent) was living with one adopted or placed child – usually with good links to the extended family. However, the children who lived in single-adult/single-child households accounted for less than a third of the sample. The majority of the children actually lived with one or more siblings.

Table 4
Composition of the households in which the children were living

No. of people in household	Frequency	Per cent
2	13	27
3	16	34
4	12	25
5	3	6
6	4	8
Totals	48	100

In most cases these siblings were also adopted, because the single people chose to adopt more than once in order to increase their family to the desired size. There were only nine single adopters who had previously had their own children, and in all but two of these cases the birth

Table 5
Numbers of children in the adoptive households

No. of children	Frequency	Per cent
1	14	29
2	20	42
3	10	21
4 or more	4	8
Totals	48	100

children were old enough to have moved out of the immediate household. The typical adopted child of a single parent was not therefore the "odd one out" in a household where nobody else was adopted, and there were no birth children close enough in age to pose a threat to the adopted child (Wedge and Mantle, 1991).

Besides the adoptive parent and his or her children, the number of people in the household includes other family members. Ten per cent of children in the sample lived in a family where there was a resident grandparent (three of these were grandmothers and two were grand-fathers). These relatives were important to the children and often helped substantially with child care.

Occupation
One-third of the adopted children in the sample were living with an adoptive parent who was professionally employed, either full-time or part-time (this includes two boys who were living with adoptive fathers).

Only one-third of the adopters (ten out of 30) were unemployed, but – as might be expected – those who did not work outside the home tended to be caring for a greater number of children. This means that about half the children in the sample were looked after by a mother who was not in paid employment.

Total household income

The situation we recorded for the single adoptive parent's occupation is reflected in the distribution of income. Children living with adopters in well-paid jobs or professions enjoyed a relatively high standard of living; but there were some very poor adoptive parents as well as others who were comparatively well off.

Some inequalities seemed to be caused by the fact that adoption allowances were not means-tested or treated as an official source of income (although they clearly performed this function) and they were not often paid to the adopters of young, undamaged black children, who were considered to fit the traditional pattern of baby adoptions and therefore did not require a subsidy. Larger allowances were attracted by white teenagers who were considered hard to place. Generally speaking the arrangements for the allocation of adoption allowances seemed patchy, and in some local authorities they were clearly in need of revision.

Housing

Three-quarters of the children in the adoptive sample were living in owner-occupied housing (Table 6). Understandably, some of the properties occupied by the single adopters were of modest size. Ten per cent of the children were living in houses or flats with three rooms in addition to kitchens or bathrooms (this would have allowed for one sitting-room/living-room if a single parent and child had a bedroom each). However, most of the children were living in houses with four or five rooms in addition to kitchens and bathrooms.

Table 6
The children's housing

Type of housing	Frequency	Per cent
Owner-occupied	36	75
Council rented	10	21
Private rented	2	4
Totals	48	100

Ethnicity

Out of the 30 adopters in the study, 11 were black women. Eight of these were of African or African-Caribbean origin and three were of mixed parentage.

A similar proportion of the children (35 per cent of the sample) had been classified by the adoption agencies as black. These 17 black children included ten of African or African-Caribbean origin and seven of mixed parentage. They had all been placed with black adopters – with the exception of two children of mixed parentage who had been placed with a white woman on the grounds that she was already bringing up the first child because of a family connection. There were no black adopters bringing up white children.

Previous experience of relationships

Nine of the adopters had previously been married. Of these, one had been widowed and the other eight had been divorced. The other 21 adopters had always had single status, although some had had temporary partnerships in the past. None of them stated that they were gay or lesbian. Also, none of the adopters had any significant disabilities.

These brief statistics say something about the characteristics of the adopters and the households in which the children were living at the time of the research. We must now unravel more of the process by which they came to be there.

Previous experiences of family living

When we consider in detail the family structures in which single adopters were brought up, two features stand out as important. Firstly, *almost none of these single applicants was an only child*. Apart from one woman whose parents separated at an early stage, they were all brought up in families where there were other children. It was also noticeable that there seemed to be a tendency for the adoptive applicant to be in the middle of the group rather than the oldest or the youngest, and in very large sibling groups the adoptive applicant was usually towards the younger end. We can only speculate about the possible significance of these family patterns, which may be accidental or related to all kinds of factors both internal and external to the family. The only safe conclusion is that because the adoptive applicants grew up in families which included children and adults of different ages, it would have seemed unnatural for them to live alone.

A second feature which linked the histories of the single female adopters was that *their own mother was usually a very important figure in their upbringing.* In many cases the grandmother had brought up her own family without the aid of a partner, either because she was widowed or divorced or because the task of child-care had been delegated to her. Even in marriages which were considered traditional and successful, the original mother had often done most of the caring. Most of the single women who were approved for adoption therefore had experience of possible role models and a clear notion of what it was feasible for them to achieve.

In both black and white families there were, of course, long-standing feuds and sources of permanent or transient irritation. In two cases where black parents had emigrated to this country during the 1960s, they had left young children to be looked after temporarily by relatives in their countries of origin. When accommodation and employment were secured and the time seemed right for the children to join their parents, the move was blocked either by relatives or by officialdom or by a mixture of the two. The women fought to regain their children and did so, but missed out on the experience of parenting during the formative years. As a result, it was only through the adoption of other children two decades later that their experience of motherhood became complete.

The influence of friends and social groups

For roughly one-quarter of the adoptive parents a religious upbringing and continuing religious beliefs were an important influence on the decision to adopt. These parents grew up with a strong social conscience, a capacity for altruism or self-denial, and a desire to help those who were vulnerable or underprivileged. This was particularly significant since the children available for single-person adoption were largely children with special needs.

For parents with religious beliefs, their faith was clearly a source of great personal strength, and one very practical benefit associated with the beliefs was that the parents had active involvement in a religious community within which they and their adopted children could find security and acceptance. For other parents in the study, their social meeting grounds were more secular in nature; but we must not under-estimate the impact they had on the desire to adopt. Women were frequently members of groups in which both adults and children were actively involved, and it seemed natural that children should attend. One adopter had a wide circle of Nigerian friends forming four different groups who met in each others' houses on a regular basis. The first of these groups consisted solely of people from the village in which she had been born. The second included people from her home town generally. The members of a third group were all Nigerian women, and those of a fourth group were simply Nigerian.

Membership of networks such as these increased the incentive to adopt, since the meetings were frequented by other parents and their children and the value attached to having children was high. Single people could feel left out, or at best marginally involved, if they did not have children themselves.

The experiences of loss which preceded the adoption
The application to adopt was always made for positive reasons, but in many cases the parents reported personal changes in the time immedi-ately preceding the application – loss of partners when the relationship had gone wrong, of family members who had died, of grown children who had moved away, or simply of spent youth. The list of missing people was not always confined to the adopters' own family members, since some single women had taken on a quasi-parental role with other people's children.

One single woman said:

> *I think what spurred me on more than anything [in relation to the adoption application] was that my friends who have three children went to Australia. I lived close by and three children were suddenly gone from my life. I had made lots of time in my life for these children.*

Another who had become involved in fostering and child-minding said:

> *I would like to have adopted Naomi [a previous foster child] but legally she was quite complicated and we only got permission to*

*adopt her at the beginning of her fifteenth year when she decided
she was leaving anyway. It was quite sad.*

For women who were interested in looking after children on a long-term
basis, a major incentive to adopt was the knowledge that it would prevent
children from being taken away. (Fostering was often rejected because it
did not offer this security.) One woman applied to adopt a Down's
Syndrome child after the death of her own infant who had been similarly
disabled. Although she had four children living with her at the time, she
was still capable of saying:

The house was empty because he wasn't there.

Another woman described a visit to some friends, at a time when her
own children were beginning to leave home.

*They're not that much older than me, and there was just the two
of them sitting there. I sort of walked into their house and I
thought 'This place is dead!' I didn't really feel that I was ready
for that phase of life.*

Not all the adopters who had had children were reacting to what is
traditionally known as an "empty nest". One black woman who had
been widowed when her two children were very small felt that she
would have liked a larger family, in common with her friends and her
sisters, and she said that if her husband had lived they would almost
certainly have had more children. She avoided taking another partner
while her children were young because she was afraid that the presence
of a stepfather would bring conflict into the family. When she discovered
that single-person adoption was possible, it provided a way for her to
increase the size of her family by adopting two young boys, thereby
matching her own expectations and coming closer to what she felt was a
cultural norm.

The experience of childlessness
Only nine out of the 30 adoptive parents in the study had had their own
children. Twenty-one parents were childless and ten of these said that
they had never had a sexual partner.

For childless women the adoption obviously had special meaning; but some distinction needs to be made between the women who had never had a partner and who therefore could reasonably assume that child-bearing would have been possible for them, and those who knew that they could not conceive or bear a child. Some of these women had tried to become pregnant and failed, or had suffered a series of miscarriages. A few had had hysterectomies. Like many married couples who find their way to adoption agencies, these women had had to come to terms with their own infertility; but in addition to this they had sometimes had to cope with desertion by the partners who had hoped for natural children by them, and who felt that in the absence of children the partnership had little meaning. Their grief at finding they were childless had often been compounded by the feeling of worthlessness, when they were abandoned in favour of a younger or more obviously fertile woman.

Again, the situation of many of the black adopters was different from that of their white counterparts. Seven out of the 11 black adopters in the sample had discovered that they were infertile, and this discovery had usually been linked to the breakdown of a partnership. Only four out of the 19 white adopters knew that they could not conceive, and in two cases where hysterectomies had been necessary for medical reasons, the operations did not carry a great deal of emotional impact because the women had no intention of ever becoming pregnant. Parenting was important to them and parenting was about looking after children. However, many of the white single women in their 40s or 50s regretted the fact that they had not had children earlier in life (they regretted the lack of children rather than the lack of partners). Some would never have considered a sexual liaison outside marriage; but a slightly greater number said that they had been restrained by social conventions which they now felt to be less important. Two white women had tried very hard to become pregnant, one by *in vitro* fertilisation (IVF) and the other by a temporary partnership in her late 30s.

Sometimes it was the very act of considering adoption that had caused a male partner to leave. One woman who had had seven miscarriages during her marriage explained how she started to consider adoption because she very much wanted a child, but it transpired that her husband 'only wanted his own'. They separated and later obtained a divorce. Another woman who had difficulty in conceiving underwent several attempts at IVF, one of which resulted in an ectopic pregnancy. Her partner was happy to co-operate with the treatment until it was discovered that he himself had a low sperm count. Because of the perceived insult to his male pride, he found that he could not handle this situation and he moved away. A third woman in the sample was deserted by her partner during the adoption process itself because he began to realise that he was not suited to the role of adoptive father. Again, he formed a liaison with a woman who seemed likely to provide him with a natural child.

It is obvious that experiences of this kind can leave a caring woman isolated from her partner by very reason of the fact that she has a strong desire to adopt. If adoption were denied to single people, a woman in this position would be denied the satisfaction of having children, through no fault of her own, and at the same time her considerable resources would be lost to children in need of care.

The importance of feminist views

The adoptive parents had not always regretted the transition to single status, even where a partnership had broken down in distressing circumstances. Several women had eased the departure of their partners or separated from them after discovering that they were incompatible, and at least one was glad to be freed from physical violence. These women understood the experiences of children who had been abused by men.

Many of the adopters had what might be described as liberal feminist views, inasmuch as they had a great respect for the values of 'sharing, caring and nurturing' (Ruyek, 1986) and wanted them to be used in child-rearing. Several of the single people who had never had partners also said that they had always been perfectly happy on their own. They embodied the qualities admired by Mary Wollstonecraft, who said in her *Vindication of the Rights of Women* (1972):

> To be a good mother a woman must have sense and that independence of mind which few women possess who are taught to depend entirely on their husbands.

A few parents acknowledged a slight sense of loss in being single even though there was no-one in particular they were grieving for, but at the same time they were also conscious of the advantages of *not* having a partner. It was seen as another relationship which both they and the child would have to cope with. Mothers caring for difficult or disabled children often felt that they would not have the resources to look after a husband as well. It is interesting that they saw the partnership in that light, but as we have mentioned already, some had actually experienced a relationship in which they did all the caring.

Another point is that because of their expectations of what marriage would mean, active single women feared the loss of valued freedoms. In spite of various demands upon their time and energies, they had been able to maintain their own occupations and interests in a way which, they felt, might be threatened by a traditional heterosexual partnership; and they had built up habits of unilateral decision-making and planning which they wanted to retain.

The relevance of employment

At the time when the applications were lodged, all but five of the prospective adopters were in full-time employment. If they were young women, they often found that friends and acquaintances were leaving work, at least temporarily, to have children. One woman who worked as a secretary in a London bank was "filling in" for someone on maternity leave at the same time as she was pursuing her own plans for adoption, and the knowledge that she was about to share in the experience of her contemporaries (albeit under different terms and conditions) was a source of pleasure. Older people in employment, on the other hand, were at a different stage in their life-cycle. They had often been absorbed in their work through years of intensive career-building, and had reached a more settled phase of life in which they were ready to enjoy some of the experiences which had been missed before.

Apart from providing friends and colleagues and facilitating the spread of ideas, the actual experience of being in employment was useful in three main ways. Firstly, it provided some applicants with a reasonable level of income so that, although adoption allowances were often necessary, they did not feel that they were approaching the agency "cap in hand". Secondly, the fact that many of the women planned to continue in employment meant that they were actively seeking a child of nursery school age or even older, so that they were automatically placing themselves in a category whose demands were likely to be satisfied. Thirdly, the experience of professional employment or care work had alerted some of them to the particular needs of abused or disabled children, and in some cases to the backgounds of children in the care system. This understanding made them highly acceptable to the adoption agency and it was particularly valuable when they were linked with difficult children.

Job opportunities were part of the picture, but actual redundancies were less important in the run-up to the adoption than a wish for a change of employment. Some parents clearly enjoyed the challenge of taking on a child who had been classified as "unadoptable", and if they lacked confidence in their own parenting skills, it was perhaps comforting to be offered a child who had "nowhere to go but up". However, very few of the adopters actually asked for a child with special needs. They saw parenting as a normal part of their life experience and they wanted life to be as normal as possible both for themselves and for their children.

The overwhelming impression is that the single people who adopted deprived and disabled children were not saints or martyrs. They could more accurately be described as pioneers. They applied to adopt older children because these were the categories of children available to them, because they felt they understood the children's needs, and because they had the personal skills and determination to persist in the face of discouragement and vastly unequal opportunities.

It is useful to reflect that 28 of the adopters were single women and 11 of them were black. In our largely heterosexual, white and male-dominated society, it is not within these groups that the main power lies.

Summary

- The single applicants in the study showed a great deal of commitment to the idea of adoption. Whether they were men or women, parenthood was central to their sense of identity.
- In 27 per cent of cases in the sample, one adult (the parent or prospective parent) was living with one adopted or placed child. However, the majority of households included other siblings who were usually also adopted.

- One-third of the children were living with an adoptive mother who was professionally employed. On the whole, the standard of living was slightly higher than average, but there were some very poor adoptive parents as well as others who were relatively well-off. Out of the 30 adopters, 11 were black women.
- In their families of origin, the adopters had not usually been "only children". They were used to living in families with adults and children of different ages. Another common feature was that, for the female adopters, their own mother had been a key figure in their upbringing.
- Friends, social groups, religion and patterns of employment all had an influence on the adopter's wish to have children.
- Many of the adopters had suffered a sense of loss resulting from infertility, broken partnerships or children moving away. However, they were mainly motivated by the desire to look after children whose needs they felt they understood. In some cases they eschewed partnerships, present or future, in favour of child-rearing.

6 The attitudes of referring agencies

Historically the recruitment or sanctioning of adoptive parents has always reflected contemporary concerns about family life (Boswell, 1988; Rapoport *et al*, 1977). Is there any evidence in the referrals from local authorities in our study that a single person was the first or only choice, when adoptive parents were sought for particular children?

Referrals from local authorities

The adoptive parents who were interviewed during the research had usually been approved by the adoption agencies, but the children with whom they were matched had been looked after for varying periods of time by local authority social services in different parts of the country. Long-term plans for these children had been formed and it was felt that they were in need of adoption. The voluntary agency which had prospective parents eager and waiting for children therefore offered a resource that the local authority wanted.

In the requests which were made to the voluntary agencies by local authorities, single adopters were very rarely sought directly. The file study revealed only one referral which actively invited the names of single applicants to be brought forward as a first priority. This request represented a change of plan, since the original intention had been to place the members of a particular sibling group together in a two-parent family. The letter of referral says:

> *When their Form Es were first completed in [date given] it was presumed we would be seeking a family to take all three children together as a sibling group. However, after a further review held on [date six months later] we have decided to place the children individually with single parents.*

Form E published by BAAF is the document which gives details of a child to be placed and makes recommendations for the type of placement.

In the above case several parts of the form had been scored out, bearing witness to recent changes in direction. Under "placement required" there was a deleted recommendation for joint placement of the siblings, and under "family structure" the original entry read as follows:

> *Two parents are necessary for this sibling group, and ideally they will be a mature couple who have already had parenting experience. Frank, Matt and Josie will require a great deal of energy, patience and nurturing.*

It is interesting that this entry was deleted. What brought about the change in direction, so that one parent was eventually sought for each child rather than two for all? Was it simply a matter of practicality – a compromise brought about by the realisation that the "mature couple with parenting experience" was unobtainable for these children? It would not be surprising if this were the case. However, the recommendations appear to have been shaped, at least in part, by a particularly sensitive assessment from the resource centre in which the children were living at the time. This report focused in detail on the individual needs of the children, and its author had clearly envisaged that their needs might best be met by single adopters. In particular it was suggested that the girl, Josie, should be placed separately from her siblings since she had an extreme need to form 'a deep and meaningful attachment to one person, perhaps with additional professional input.' At the same time it was seen as important that she should keep in contact with her brothers when she was placed. The report concluded:

> *These very special needs could most suitably be met by a single, mature woman who has no other children, but who has a strong support system of her own to cope with the rejections she may face. I feel that the carer will need to have a central maternalistic drive, without traditional illusions about motherhood, in order to appreciate Josie's considerable strengths and potential.*

It is a tribute to the success of the family-finding process that a single woman with exactly these qualities was found to parent Josie, and that one of the girl's siblings was adopted by another single parent in the study. (The eldest child lingered for a while in the residential home, but he too has now been moved to an adoptive placement.) Previously, in the birth family, these children had clung together for survival. They were seen as an undifferentiated group by their parents and by some of the people who had looked after them subsequently. Through separate placements with single people their individual needs have had a chance of being met, and because of the adopters' sensitivity to the underlying family situation, an appropriate level of contact between the siblings has been maintained.

This is a fascinating case with a great many reverberations, many of which are concerned with the relationship between adoption and family structure. Apart from the single parent issue, it raises questions about how local authorities may best respond to the spirit of the law, when considering the requirement to place siblings together 'so far as is reasonably practical and consistent with their welfare' (Children Act 1989, Section 23.7b). Ten years ago, Triseliotis commented on the need to keep sibling groups together and not to allow them to be divided on placement 'for sheer administrative convenience', but he saw the preservation of the group as being more necessary in residential care than in adoption because of the quality of nurturing available to the children, and he also maintained that the ill-effects of division could be alleviated if attempts were made to maintain the links between the siblings (Triseliotis and Russell, 1984). More recent research has explored the relationships between brothers and sisters in the care system in greater detail, and in general it supports the joint placement of siblings wherever possible. However, suggestions have also been made that 'proactive ways of working with siblings should be developed by social work practitioners and carers', and that the focus of this work could be the children's separate experiences as well as those which are shared (Kosonen, 1994).

From the point of view of our study, the really interesting point to note is that, as a result of an imaginative assessment, a group of single people was considered capable of parenting individual children and at the same time maintaining the integration of the sibling network, yet single-person adoption was not a first choice of the referring agency. In fact it was assumed that these children's needs would best be met by joint placement in a conventional family structure. It was only when the children's needs were disaggregated, without actually losing sight of the wider perspective, that the viability of single-person adoption was understood.

On a more general level still, the old and the new judgements in this case stand at the meeting point of two adoption paradigms. Both are concerned with the quality of parenting and in that sense they overlap, but the paradigm based on automatic respect for orthodox family structure has given way to one which has at its centre the psychological development of an individual child.

Issues of gender and sexuality

The referral mentioned above was unusual in recommending adoption by a single person, even after a second consideration of the issues. It was also unusual inasmuch as it did not discriminate between men and women. The initial letter invited queries from both male and female applicants.

Normally it seemed to be assumed not only that a single applicant would be a second choice to a couple, but that any successful single applicant would be a *woman*. One senior adoption officer who had been approached about the approval of a single male applicant replied:

> *We have no policy about single men, but of course we would want to look very carefully should we have one put forward for one of our children. The adoption panel would like to discuss any suggested link [between parent and child] as a matter of principle at an early stage.*

According to present practice it appears not only that single adopters are viewed less favourably than couples, but that single men are considered less eligible than single women. The conclusion seems to be that women are more fitted than men to perform a caring role, but that they can function best in the context of a heterosexual partnership.

Sometimes gender matching of parent and child appeared to be indicated in the referrals, and there were good reasons for this recommendation (such as the provision of adult role models). The sibling group referred to above contained boys as well as girls, and this is probably why both male and female applicants were being sought, but it would still have been possible – and by no means unusual – to give priority to the applications of single women. A child placement consultant who had been sent the papers of a single man felt that the applicant had 'a great deal to offer to the right child', but she added the following perceptive comment to her report:

> *It seems appropriate only to consider him for boys, whereas it is quite usual to consider single women adopters for boys as well as girls. Given that there are no legal bars, it just shows how complex our attitudes are to gender and sexuality issues.*

One of the attitudes in question may be the belief that women are less likely to commit sexual abuse. There are of course women who violate children's sexual boundaries, and recent research has highlighted their problems and case histories (Saradjian, 1996), but it is still true that the majority of sexual abusers are men.

None of the women in the study were lesbians, even though adoption by a lesbian couple would ensure that the child has two carers. Prejudice against homosexuality is known to be widespread (Kitzinger, 1987), and one of the obstacles to the approval of single people as adopters may be the fear of inadvertently selecting someone who is not heterosexual. One of the single adopters in the study said:

> *People always worry about my sexual orientation. It's one of the first things they think about.*

The right of a social services department to seek an adoption order for a child living with a lesbian carer was recently challenged in court, and defended [*Re W* (Adoption: Homosexual Adopter) Family Division, 11 April 1997]. In spite of this, it seems that known lesbians and gay men are not often selected as adoptive parents in the United Kingdom. None was met in the course of the study, although the pieces of research so far conducted on these issues suggest that the sexual orientation of the parent will make little difference to a child's development (Green *et al*, 1986; Gottman, 1989; Brown, 1991). The pressure to exclude homosexuals must make it more difficult for a single man to be approved as an adoptive parent, unless his views about sexuality are both orthodox and absolutely clear.

Attitudes to gender and sexuality in adoption probably do need to be explored. One hopes that in the approval process most potential abusers will be screened out, but if sexual abuse is feared, it does not help to select children of the same sex as a male carer, since confirmed paedophiles have been known to make no distinction between pre-pubertal boys and girls.

For whatever reason, there are only two single male adopters in the study. One applicant was already caring for a young boy who had been placed with him and his former wife before his marriage broke up, and he reported considerable difficulty in obtaining permission to adopt as a single person in spite of the fact that he had already been approved as a potential father. At one stage the local authority had threatened to withdraw the child and place him in foster care. These difficulties are more surprising in view of the fact that the child had formed a strong bond with his carer, after a previous history of foster placement breakdowns, and the prospective adopter's situation might be considered one of the 'small number of exceptional circumstances' which are seen as readily permissible in the government's White Paper, *Adoption: The future* (DoH and Welsh Office, 1993).

> *There may, too, be a small number of other exceptional circumstances where adoption by a single person may be sensible – for example a widowed step-father with whom the child has already lived before the mother's death.*

If divorce is substituted for the mother's death, the parallels in the above situation become clear. However, a major consideration in this single adopter's case was that at the time of the marriage break-up the child had not formally been adopted. If it had not been for administrative delays, the situation would probably have been dealt with under private law and problems need never have arisen.

The other male applicant, who had never been married, had spent several years in a caring profession and was described in the Schedule 2 Report as having 'outstanding ability to relate to children'. Nevertheless the social worker who conducted the assessment told him that he might have to wait a long time for a child, with no guarantee of success at the end of it.

Because of his 'outstanding ability' the man referred to above was actually approved and had a young boy placed with him within a year of his assessment by the adoption agency, which in relation to the usual speed of adoptions is extremely rapid progress. Once again the matching appears to have been done by an intelligent disaggregation of the child's needs and a realisation that they could be met in an unconventional family structure. The dominant themes in the assessment (attachment, bonding, security and emotional growth) were those of developmental psychology. One highly significant feature of the adoption, however, was that the boy was still in touch with his birth mother and sister, and it was intended that face-to-face contact would continue. It was hoped that the birth mother would look more favourably on the adoption if she was not to be replaced by another female carer. To the courts and the outside world, too, it may be reassuring to know that when a single man becomes an adoptive parent, the child's mother and sister can continue to exercise a female caring role.

Specific recommendations about family structure
As previously mentioned, very few recommendations for single-person adopters of either sex were made at the referral stage. Apart from a few ambiguously worded statements in which the word "adopter" has an "s" added in brackets so that the request would apply either to couples or to single people, the assumption seemed to be that two heterosexual parents would be chosen.

It could be argued that requests at this stage are necessarily imprecise in order to allow for flexibility in the matching process. Nevertheless details about preferred family structure did occur on the Form Es, but these recommendations very rarely mentioned parents. The requests tended to concentrate on the presence or absence of possible siblings. The issue here was not primarily contact with birth siblings, although this relationship was clearly important and – as in the case already quoted at the start of this chapter – it might be an additional feature of the adoption. What was under scrutiny was the child's possible member-ship of a household in which there were already children (either adopted or non-adopted) who would become brothers and sisters for the newly adopted child.

Requests for siblings

Sometimes it appeared that the referring social worker wanted the new child to have the benefit of sibling companionship with a minimum of sibling rivalry. When other children are present in the household the situation becomes more complicated and there may well be conflict. This is probably one of the reasons why, in the 1960s, many of the adoption agencies demanded that successful applicants should show some proof of infertility (Goodacre, 1966.) However, subsidiary factors such as the age differences between children in substitute placements are important, as some classic research studies have shown. A study by Parker in the 1960s found that the factor most detrimental to successful foster care was the presence of the carers' own children, especially if they were young and near the age of the foster child (Parker, 1966). Another study by Trasler demonstrated that failure rates were noticeably higher when foster carers had a child of their own who was of the same sex and within three years of age of the foster child (Trasler, 1960). In general terms, the link between foster placement breakdown and the presence of the carers' own children was demonstrated again by George (1970) and by Berridge and Cleaver (1987). Other more recent research has suggested that in order to minimise the risk of placement breakdown, the placed child should be younger than any new step-sibling by at least three years (Wedge and Mantle, 1991).

Since there is no evidence that adoption is exempt from the risks which are common in foster care, the findings of these studies seem to militate against the placement of children in situations where the carers have offspring of their own. However, the arrangements involving step-siblings which have caused most concern and which have generally been the subject of research are situations where the new child is placed alongside the birth children of the adoptive parents. These "natural" children have a different status and enjoy a favoured position in the household. When all the children in the household are adopted, status differences based on genealogy seem less likely to exist. In fact Trasler (1960) found that some of the most *favourable* circumstances in foster care were those where another foster child, either related or unrelated, was present in the household. Single people who have no children of their own and who adopt more than once in order to create a family have a clear advantage here.

Sometimes the concerns expressed in the referrals we examined were about the child's relationship with future siblings. More frequently, however, the social worker who prescribed certain sibling groupings was concerned about the child's relationship with the prospective *adopter*, and the way in which this relationship might be helped or hindered by the presence of other children. In the referrals there were frequent recommendations which suggested that in order to achieve a parent–child relationship of sufficient intensity, the adopted child needed to be the eldest or only child in the family. On a couple of occasions, however, it was claimed that a child who had had too much responsibility for younger children in the birth family would benefit from the protection of an older brother or sister, in order to experience a more normal childhood.

Given the range and variety of single-adult households, these recommendations do not rule out single applicants and sometimes actually favour them. Prospective adoptive parents who have no partner, who are mature and stable and in some cases beyond child-bearing age, are likely to have abandoned the idea of procreation and may be happy to commit themselves to bringing up a single vulnerable child. On the other hand those who adopt more than once may provide the newly adopted child with an older sibling who is also adopted and enjoys a similar status in the household. Single mothers who already have children by a previous relationship can be seen as fitting either category of need, if (as happened in the study) their children are grown-up and independent or on the point of leaving home but maintaining close relationships with the family. In the accounts which were given to us by parents and children, these older non-adopted siblings served variously as adult role models, protectors, advocates and companions for the adopted child.

Requests for structural matching
There are some other references to family structure in the referrals which are of interest, since they form part of the background to the adoptions by single people and they also indicate the features of family placements that local authority social workers deemed to be important.

The forms occasionally contain references to existing structures in the birth family or in the foster family. The implication is that structural matching is required, and the aim of matching in these cases is *to make the transition easier*. For example, the details provided for one small girl included the comment:

> She will move easily into a home with other children, as she is used to having both an older sister and a younger brother in the foster home.

These arguments for choosing a particular family structure on grounds of ease of transition were apparently given some attention when discussions about matching were entered into. However, there were often considerable differences between the adoptive homes and the foster homes children had previously lived in, because the foster homes had two parents and a greater number of children. It was also obvious that the child's passage was eased successfully, in most cases, not primarily by attempts to match family structures but by a carefully graded programme of introductions and preparation for the adoption.

In short, direct references to family structure at the time when a child is referred for adoption are vague, and in most cases they do not provide an adequate explanation of why single applicants have been chosen. When single people have been selected as adoptive parents, we have to look closely at the needs of the children they are required to parent. It is also useful to bear in mind that there is a strong element of *self*-selection, which ensures that prospective parents apply for – and in most cases receive – the kind of children who match their interests, sympathies, caring abilities and professional skills. However, the scales are not evenly balanced.

The pressure of "market forces"

Older children who have suffered abusive and developmentally damaging experiences are not easy to place for adoption. To put it crudely, they have a low level of "marketability". Reference has already been made to the kind of assessment which can lead to the positive selection of a single carer within the paradigm of developmental psychology. In the documents available on file, however, there are frequent indications that although the single person who was eventually chosen had all the skills and qualities necessary to parent the child, *a single person was not actually selected until the search to find a couple had proved fruitless.* The referral statement and the documented actions of the local authority in such cases reflect the assumption that two parents are necessary for adoption, and the best possible outcome for the child is adoption by a "mature couple", with or without parenting experience. Because of the pressure of market forces, however, it was necessary to look elsewhere if two parents with the necessary skills were not available.

One addendum to a Schedule 2 Report speaks of an 'exhaustive search' which was made to find a couple capable of adopting an 11-year-old boy before he was placed with a single mother. Since the local authority had no suitable family available, his details were circulated nationally through various channels which included the BAAF Regional Exchange and plentiful advertising both in specialist journals and in ordinary newspapers. He was even featured in *Farmers' Weekly* because of his expressed interest in farms and animals. But 'the response to advertising was negligible'. In another case involving a nine-year-old girl who had behaviour problems and learning difficulties, it was reported that a total of 57 families had been explored prior to the selection of the single woman who adopted her.

Addenda to Schedule 2 Reports, which are a good source of this type of information, were requested by judges who had doubts about the thoroughness of the family-finding process. The arguments contained in the reports may have been designed to fit the judge's known or suspected prejudices, but nevertheless it is staggering to discover that so many other families (presumably mostly two-parent families) were given at least some consideration as a first priority, and either withdrew or were rejected before a single-person placement was made. If this history was known, it must have contributed to a feeling of "less eligibility" on the part of less confident adopters, and the delay in finding an adoptive home for a child, together with its accompanying frustrations, may also have increased the risk that children would be slow to trust and would "test out" the placement with bad behaviour.

The longer the waiting time, the more difficult it must have been for worried and rootless children to believe that a permanent family would ever be found.

Summary

- The referrals from local authorities suggest that single adopters are less sought-after than couples, and single men are considered less eligible than single women.

- None of the single adopters in the sample were lesbians or homosexuals. Attitudes to gender and sexuality in adoption do need to be explored.

- The single adopters in this study usually had no natural children close in age to the adopted child. It is an advantage to know that in these households all children will have adoptive status.

- With the help of developmental psychologists, imaginative assessments are possible. For example, a group of single people may be considered capable of parenting individual members of a sibling group and maintaining the contact between the children.

- Family structure was seldom specified in the requests made by local authorities to the adoption agencies. It seemed to be assumed that two heterosexual parents would be chosen. However, there were sometimes detailed recommendations about sibling groupings, and structural matching was advocated to make the transition easier.

- The documents on file suggest that although the single adopters had all the skills necessary to parent these children, they were often not approved by the local authorities until a search to find two parents had proved fruitless. This must have caused delay, which in some cases could have been harmful.

7   Experiences of the approval process

When the single people in the study approached an adoption agency with a request to be considered for a child, they were taking action to implement a personal decision that had been taken in private, usually after discussion with only a few close friends and relatives, and often after a good deal of heart-searching. They had arrived at the adoption agency by a number of different routes, some of which were circuitous.

Table 7
Source of the information which initiated interest in single-person adoption

Information source	No. of adopters (N=30)
Newspaper advertisement	10
Professional contact	7
Informal sources	6
Agency enquiry	4
Television advertisement	3

Sources of initial information

Thirteen people (43 per cent of the adult sample) had been introduced to the idea of single-person adoption by means of an advertisement, usually in a newspaper such as *The Voice* or *The Guardian* but occasionally on television. Another 13 applicants learned about it from friends, family members or colleagues, and the remainder contacted an agency directly.

Seven people in the sample first encountered the information in a professional context because they worked in social services or an agency which was closely allied to it. Two of these people were social workers, two were teachers of children with special needs, and another three worked for statutory or voluntary welfare agencies. All but one of these adopters were white.

It is interesting to note that the information which was employment based did not spread readily beyond a rather restricted network. For example, none of the health service workers learned about single-person adoption through their work contacts, regardless of the level of the organisation on which they were employed. One senior health manager heard about the possibilities on television. One nurse and one health visitor, both of whom were black, responded to a newspaper advertisement, and another white health visitor obtained the information from family and friends.

In all, six people became interested after hearing about adoption from informal sources. Two of them had adopters among their family members. These people were among the most interested and the most committed of those who made an initial enquiry, since they already had first-hand knowledge of adoption and were convinced of its value; paradoxically, their approach was less easy.

The people who did not see or respond to an advertisement had no clear avenue of approach, and they usually started by contacting either their local authority or BAAF. From there, they were redirected to one of the voluntary adoption agencies. The applicants sometimes had to go by way of the local authority and *then* BAAF before they were given the address of an agency (a cumbersome three-stage approach).

The timing of the application
The information that people acquired from advertisements or by word of mouth was not always acted on immediately. In several cases it lay dormant until the adopters probed their own feelings, or plucked up enough courage to approach an adoption agency. Conversely, newspaper and television advertising could act as a trigger in cases where people already knew about the possibility of single-person adoption and were at least partly committed to it, although they had previously taken no action. The impact of any advertisement varied enormously, depending on where it fell in the adopter's chronological and emotional time-scale.

A surprising number of people (more than half the sample) had been attracted to the notion of adoption for some time without realising that it was an option which was available to them, or without having the courage to pursue it. One parent said that she had been thinking about it on and off for ten years. Another woman who adopted three children in succession said that when she first heard of single-person adoption she thought that it was a 'daft idea'. Among the black adopters there was a woman who noted down the agency's name and telephone number on the back of a magazine, when she saw a programme on television one evening. She did nothing about it at the time, but she kept the magazine and applied two years later. Similarly one of the two male adopters was interested enough to 'cut something out of a newspaper' some years previously, but he felt that he could not apply because 'it was not the done thing'.

These responses suggest that the prospective parents were facing an information hurdle, combined with apprehension about the legitimacy of adopting as a single person. The timing of most applications was clearly linked to the personal circumstances of the adopters, and this process could not be hurried, but some applications would undoubtedly have been made sooner if the parents had had more information. The anticipation of social stigma deterred them in two ways: firstly, by making it more difficult for single people with conventional attitudes to apply, and secondly, by creating the impression that adoption regulations are more rigid than is actually the case.

Preconceptions and misconceptions of the criteria

Just over half the applicants who responded to an advertisement as their first line of approach were surprised to learn that single people were not necessarily excluded, since they had assumed that only couples could be accepted. A few of these parents also feared that there would be other requirements such as commitment to a religious faith. A professional woman with extensive experience of child care believed for some time that because she was not a church member adoption would not be open to her.

Like the white applicants, black single women reported that they had harboured anxieties about the acceptability of their marital status and religion. However, there were also some fears of racial discrimination on the part of agencies, and those applicants who had a low level of material resources were inclined to think that they would be ruled out by financial and housing requirements. One black parent spoke of her initial worries as follows:

> My concept of adoptive parents was that they should be rich, middle class, with a huge house and pots of money and – obviously – married.

These ideas are quite understandable, given prevailing stereotypes and the history of adoption policy and practice. At the time when Iris Goodacre carried out her survey in the 1960s, all adoptive applicants had to be married, and only one of the ten adoption societies operating in her survey areas would consider accepting applicants without a religion. Seven of the ten societies demanded that successful applicants should be practising members of their faith, which meant that they had to attend church regularly (Goodacre, 1966).

None of the adoption agencies in the present study made religion a requirement for applicants, and material circumstances were considered less important than parenting skills.

The approval process

New applicants soon gathered that there were two parts to the approval: first of all the generalised assessment and selection endorsed by the adoption panel, which aimed not only to screen out unsuitable applicants but to prepare people for the adoption, and then the matching with an individual child. (Sometimes these two stages were carried out in tandem.) In spite of the element of self-selection, both were seen as hurdles to be overcome. There was a difference in the way people viewed them, however. Some parents – particularly those who were new to the system – believed that the initial approval was the bigger of the two hurdles, and that once this was over they were "home and dry". Others felt that nothing of real importance had happened until a child's name was linked with theirs.

Each of the three agencies studied had their own particular ways of working, but they all expected applicants to attend pre-adoption meetings or "workshops" in addition to undergoing a detailed individual assessment (usually referred to as a "home study" although it also included police checks and the collection of medical reports). It is interesting to note the single parents' experiences of these events.

Group meetings

Attendance at group meetings provided single applicants with their first taste of publicity. One parent who had been approved several years ago gave this account of a preliminary meeting to which she had been invited:

> *They were all sat in this big room and it was like – man, woman, empty chair; man, woman, empty chair. And then I was sat down on my own. Somebody said to me 'Couldn't your husband come, then?' And I said, 'Well, I'm not married.' 'Oh, goodness, you'll never get a child if you're only single.'*

The accounts of more recent experiences suggest that it would now be unusual for a single woman to find herself alone in a group of applicants who were all married or had permanent partners. However, this does not necessarily make for an easy time. Other members of the group are reported to have asked penetrating questions with an underlying competitive edge, and the group interaction was probably noted as part of the assessment process.

The workshops were often considered by the single applicants to be linked primarily to assessment and selection, although it is clear that they included a large measure of preparation for the adoption. Where applicants were uncommitted, the workshops gave them a chance to obtain the necessary information and withdraw without entering the home study; where applicants wished to continue, they became part of a community of prospective adoptive parents. In other words, the applicants were encouraged to form a kind of informal support group which was capable of sustaining them throughout the adoption process and in some cases beyond it. This probably lessened the risk of over-dependence on agency staff and at the same time ensured that the group itself had some normative force.

The more that pressures to conform existed within the group, however, the more important it was that the interests of single people and others who found themselves in a minority should be protected. Arguably it was not enough for group members simply to avoid introducing discrimination in the meetings. They needed to counteract feelings of "less eligibility" where these existed, and mitigate the effects of any discrimination which had been experienced in the world outside. Some single applicants were supremely confident and enjoyed the workshops; but others were sensitive even to slight indications of unfair questioning. What could help or hinder their integration?

Avoiding discrimination in the group

One positive feature was a good representation of personal and social characteristics and a range of ethnicities among the social workers as well as the applicants. Since nearly all the workers were women and many of them were single, it was usually fairly easy for them to relate to single female applicants. (The lack of male workers could have been a problem for male applicants, but they did not comment on it.) In one agency in particular, the black adopters appreciated the fact that there were African-Caribbean and Asian social workers who were active in looking after their interests. At the same time, the fact that white and non-white professionals were seen to be working together in a relationship of equality made the applicants feel that they had a right to be considered on the same terms as everyone else. On the other hand it seemed to be generally accepted that most social workers were middle class. It is impossible to tell whether any variation in this pattern would have encouraged the recruitment of adopters from working-class backgrounds.

Apart from a necessary attention to balance in the composition of the group, and sensitivity in the way in which introductions were handled, much depended on the selection of topics for discussion. The use of a systems approach made it possible for single people and couples to be assessed on a more equal footing, and there were some regularly discussed topics (such as the availability of substitute child care and social supports) which were clearly relevant for everyone to consider, but it was unfortunate if they were presented in such a way that single people appeared to be special targets.

Referring to the issues raised by social workers at her workshop, one single adopter said:

They weren't geared to single parents. They were based on a two-parent family and a heterosexual couple at that. There were times when I felt really angry.

The source of her anger was not so much the questions themselves as the fact that when they were addressed to married or cohabiting couples, they tended to elicit standard answers which were apparently accepted by the other people present and not fully explored. One highly relevant question put to members of the group was on the topic of how they would cope with child-care during a period of illness. Women who were married usually replied – somewhat complacently in the eyes of this single parent – that their partners would step in to help and if necessary take time off work to look after the children. She commented:

How many families does that happen in? ... There was an assumption that couples work the way we know couples don't *work.*

Other married women were apparently allowed to say that their mother would come 'from Timbuktu or somewhere' in order to look after the children in an emergency. The single parent mentioned above felt that for her the rules were much tighter, since she actually had to rack her brains and think of realistic solutions.

The feeling of being subject to different rules as a result of being single was reported by another applicant to a different agency. She was a black woman with a school-age child and she found it difficult to attend all of the evening meetings. She gave this account of what happened one evening when she telephoned the social worker to say that she could not attend.

I said I was sorry – I couldn't keep the appointment. I got the impression that she didn't really want to know. It was the feeling of 'Oh, can't you make a special effort to get to us?' And one thing sort of bothered me. I felt that had the husband of Mrs Jones or Mrs Brown rung up and said, 'My wife is not able to keep the appointment', that would have carried a lot more weight.

We do not know whether this situation was accurately perceived, but we do know that the woman experienced discouragement and that the feeling of "less eligibility" was there.

What was appreciated?
Different aspects of the workshops were appreciated for different reasons. The applicants liked watching informative films or videos, and they particularly welcomed the opportunity to talk to people who had previously adopted children with special needs (see also Kerrane *et al*, 1980). One woman had a vivid recollection of a conversation with someone who had adopted a particularly difficult child, because this person said that she had 'gone through five childminders in the first year'. The new applicant had found this conversation useful. It focused her mind on sorting out her leave arrangements, she said, because she did not have the time or energy to 'go out and look for five childminders'.

Straightforward information giving, which formed the central focus of all the early group work in one agency, was always appreciated. Applicants were interested to know about the children available for adoption. They were also glad to be given information about the legal process, and were surprised to discover, in the words of one parent, 'how long and complicated it was, and what a phenomenal amount of paperwork was involved'. However, if the meetings had a definite educational focus and the approach used was very didactic, the group could divide itself into initiated and uninitiated members, with the result that those approved as adoptive parents became judgemental or patronising towards the others. One adoptive parent said, somewhat harshly though perhaps with justification:

> *I talk to people that phone me up when they're just starting and I get very frustrated. I think 'God, was I ever that naïve?'. Did I ever think things were going to fall into my lap like these people do?*

General discussions in the workshops were capable of contributing to both learning and assessment, but their main benefit often seemed to lie in the fact that they helped to cement relationships in the group. One adopter said:

> *It was nice being with "warts and all" sorts of people. There was*

just a philosophy about the agency, that there's a parent for every child. Somehow it didn't matter so much what vulnerabilities you had. They needed to consider them in finding the right child for you.

Other single people appreciated the lack of pressure when it came to matching, and the feeling that they would not be ruled out if they turned down a child who seemed inordinately difficult.

I did feel there was a choice and that I was allowed to say 'No' to one child without any pressure being placed on me.

One applicant who had withdrawn still retained a considerable affection for the people she had met in her workshop.

If I were the agency, I would have gone right out and got a whole bunch of kids and handed them round . . . There was just a whole mixed bag of people, and they struck me, each and every one of them, as wonderful people that really wanted to do whatever they could to have a child.

The fact that she had been accepted as a member of the group helped her to face the fact that she was not classed as an adoptive parent, without loss of self-esteem.

The prospect of becoming a parent stirs up deep feelings in those who apply to adopt and not everyone can withdraw without damage. Nevertheless there were some suggestions that single people who were keen to adopt and who might possibly have succeeded, given appropriate encouragement, were deterred by group pressure and the intensity of the initial screening. Since we were able to interview very few of those who withdrew, unfortunately, we do not know how common this experience was.

Individual assessment

The single people accepted the necessity for detailed assessment on an individual basis. They seemed to expect it, and some of the older women clearly believed that the psychodynamic method of assessment (which was particularly common during the 1960s and 1970s) was not simply the dominant model but the only one to have significance. One applicant who was a health visitor said that she welcomed the interviews because 'that was what it was all about'. In regular meetings with a social worker the applicants allowed their personal background and material circumstances to be explored. The questioning was frequently found to be harrowing. Nevertheless people appeared to appreciate the reasons why it was done and they *learnt* from it. Some representative comments were as follows.

> *You obviously have to search inside yourself and look at yourself, at what you've done and how you're going to react to things – and how you were parented.*

> *It delved really deep down into your personal life, which I had not really talked to anybody about, after my divorce. It was like opening a lot of wounds.*

> *The whole process is there to make you understand yourself – to make you really ask 'What am I doing?' and 'Why am I doing this?'.*

> *There's lots of questions that are quite painful really, and I think if you haven't looked at them previously it can perhaps open doors that you hadn't thought of.*

One single woman reported that she had actually been abandoned by her partner during the course of a home study with another agency. They had intended to adopt as a couple; but after the initial interviews with a social worker he became 'disgruntled and very inward-looking'. He realised that he was incapable of adopting and after a short time he moved away. This led directly to the woman's application to adopt as a single person.

Tact and sensitivity on the part of social workers during the home study was very much valued. It was also appreciated when the discussions looked forwards as well as backwards. One parent said that her worker had been 'very sensitive about relationships, and what would happen to you after you adopted', by which she meant that they had considered the possible impact on the adopted child if the woman should form another partnership. An open style of questioning was appreciated because it left the initiative with the parent. For example, a woman who had previously experienced a cot death was asked, 'Is there anything you couldn't face in adopting a child?'. This gave her the opportunity to say 'I couldn't face it if the child died on me', and it was agreed that the application should be focused on older children.

In all three agencies, the applicants were encouraged to develop realistic preferences and take responsibility for their own decisions. Both in the pre-adoption workshops and in the home study there was extensive discussion about the type of child who would most readily fit the resources the applicant was offering, so that by the time the report went to panel, specific recommendations could be made about the age and sex of the child, about proposed ethnic or cultural background, and about the sort of disability which might be successfully dealt with.

Approximate groupings of adopters

Roughly speaking, the single adopters whom we interviewed can be divided into three groups. Firstly, there were the younger parents – women in their late 20s or early 30s without pre-existing children or specialist child-care experience, who nevertheless had a tremendous amount to offer a child in terms of warmth and security, commitment and enthusiasm. Even if the adopted child was of school age, these parents were capable of seeing the adoption in terms of a substitute birth. They spoke of 'feeling broody', and of being tremendously excited at the first meeting.

Secondly, there were older parents who had usually been married or had a permanent partner, and who had been widowed or divorced. Since they often had adult children and occasionally grandchildren, they were less excited at the prospect of the child's arrival. They believed that they could care for a deprived child, and they sought an opportunity to use the skills which they felt they had acquired through bringing up their own children. In the process, they hoped to continue an activity that they enjoyed.

Thirdly, there was the group of adopters who might be described as "professional". They were single people who felt that their work experience was directly relevant to the adoption and who wanted to care for a child in the intimate one-to-one relationship which parental responsibility would provide. They did see themselves as "mothers" or "fathers", but the important point about the adoption was that it gave them the opportunity to care for a damaged child whose needs they understood.

For ease of identification, I have called these three groups the *novices*, the *old hands* and the *professionals*. It would be wrong to classify the parents too rigidly; but nevertheless the groups are sufficiently homogeneous to be recognisable, and if occasional reference is made to these groupings it may help us to track the single applicants' experiences of the adoption and its aftermath.

Table 8
Classification of the adopters according to previous experience

	Black adopters	White adopters	Total (N30)
Novices	4	3	7
Old hands	3	4	7
Professionals	4	12	16

Summary
- Many adopters waited for some time before making the initial application. They were facing an information hurdle, combined with doubts about the legitimacy of single-person adoption.
- There were many misconceptions about the adoption criteria. In the beginning, some single people had feared that they would be ruled out on grounds of ethnicity, lack of religion, housing or financial circumstances in addition to marital status.
- Once they had made contact with the agency, the applicants were invited to attend group meetings or "workshops" in addition to individual sessions with a social worker. In spite of the delicacy and sometimes painfulness of the discussions, the individual sessions were generally welcomed.

- Group meetings were valued if they involved information sharing and companionship, but formal discussions and experiential activities were capable of creating anxiety in single applicants who were not confident about speaking in public. The feeling of being under public assessment with married couples created some strain.
- For the purposes of this study, three groupings of prospective adopters have been identified on the basis of their previous experience. They have been called the *novices*, the *old hands* and the *professionals*.
- In all three agencies, the applicants were encouraged to develop realistic preferences and to take responsibility for their own decisions. By the end of the approval process specific recommendations could be made about the age and sex of the proposed child, about ethnic or cultural background, and about the sort of disabilities which might be sucessfully dealt with.

8   Linking and placement patterns

The approval process outlined in the previous chapter was followed by a period of waiting, punctuated by considerable activity. Generally speaking the agencies hoped to bring together children and suitable parents as soon as possible. If prospective parents were approved but left without children they became frustrated, and since the assessment was not without financial cost, the agencies' precious resources were depleted unnecessarily if no adoption took place. For these reasons the actions of the agency had a tendency to accelerate once the direction was clear. Some parents were selected and approved for particular children, so that a separate matching process was unnecessary. In other cases the approval and the linking were done in separate but consecutive stages.

Experiences of the linking process
The people who were approached about particular children were generally well pleased, as it usually meant that a good match had been found. Alternatively, and sometimes additionally, the prospective adopters wrote their own letters to local authorities. The replies they received were often negative and very brief, for example, 'Two parents are required for this child'. Worse still, some letters were completely ignored, and highly committed women found themselves hoping for a particular child whose photograph they had seen at a time when the child had actually been placed elsewhere.

Up till now the assessment had concentrated on key aspects of the applicant's personality, background and family lifestyle. From this predominantly psychological arena the discussions now moved out into a situation of negotiation and bargaining. There developed a kind of modified market culture which seemed to be characteristic of the period immediately prior to the decision about placement.

This culture was not permanent. The fact that it changed later is illustrated by the reaction of one parent who, some time after the adoption, encountered another woman who claimed to have seen her child's photograph while 'looking through the journals'. With surprise and a certain amount of indignation, the adoptive mother said, 'What do you mean, "*looking through*"?'. Although it had seemed natural enough at the time, it had suddenly become intolerable to her that her daughter had been subject to this very public appraisal.

During the last stages of the pre-adoption period some of the parents clearly felt that they were caught up in a competitive situation, and that it was a sellers' market. They felt this even when the resources they were offering were in short supply. One black woman who wanted to adopt a girl, and who hoped that she might be given a young child who was black or of mixed parentage, said:

> *Girls that come through go so quick. People out there who are going for adoption have got this thing about girls . . . Everybody thinks little girls are so easy to handle. Probably sometimes they're not; they can be just as little terrors as boys. But it's mostly boys that come in for adoption.*

Another woman who had been allowed to adopt an affectionate baby with Down's Syndrome, several years ago, considered herself to be very fortunate.

> *If I applied for one now, I probably wouldn't be so lucky. There are so many people after them now.*

Information of this kind was spread throughout the parent network by word of mouth, for example, when adopters met during the annual "adoption picnic". Whether or not the rumours about the availability of certain children were true (and in some cases it is difficult to pin down the evidence which would substantiate them) they were capable of exerting a powerful influence over future choices.

Arrangements made for the children

All the children placed with the single people in the study were classified as having special needs. Out of the 48 children who were placed in new families, 22 were older white children, many of whom had a background of abuse, neglect, parental rejection or considerable disruption. Of the others, 16 were black children or children of mixed parentage who were deemed to need a placement suited to their cultural needs. The remaining ten were physically disabled or had severe learning disabilities, and all but one of them had Down's Syndrome.

Potentially, the term "special needs" could cover a multitude of problems, but in fact the categories used by the referring agencies were surprisingly discrete, with very little overlap. There were very few children whose identified needs spanned the official categories. Chief among them were three children with learning disabilities. Two of them, both white, had been physically maltreated in the past, while the third was of mixed parentage. It is interesting to note that in the placement of the first two children the need which was targeted was the learning disability, but in the placement of the third, the dominant consideration appeared to be ethnicity.

Table 9
Children's special needs

Main need identified prior to placement	No. of children (% of sample) N = 48	Average age at placement	Average no. of years in household	Average age at time of research
Emotional/ behavioural	22 (46%)	8	3	11
Cultural	16 (33%)	2	4	6
Disability	10 (21%)	3	7	10

Age at placement
The ages of the children in the sample ranged from a few months to 17 years, but it was unusual for a child to be adopted from birth. Only 15 out of the 48 children were placed during the first twelve months of life. Eleven of these were black children or children of mixed parentage, while the other four were disabled. The average age at placement, for children of all types, was between four and five years, but there was a great deal of variation.

Table 9 shows the average age at placement for the children in each special need group, together with the average number of years they had spent in the household and the average age at the time of our interviews. The black children and the disabled children were the youngest at the time of placement, but the disabled children had been in their placements for slightly longer when our interviews were held. This appears to reflect a pattern of allocation during the mid or late 1980s, when a number of children with Down's Syndrome were placed with single women, many of whom were widows with grown children of their own.

During this period and immediately following it, an increasing number of black children were placed with single carers by IAS and the Thomas Coram Foundation. The most recently placed children, however, tended to be the older, white children, some of whom had entered their adoptive families very shortly before our interviews.

The parents in the study were older than one might expect of new parents. Their ages when a child was placed with them ranged from 27 to 54 years, and the average age at the time of placement was around 40. When seen in relation to the age of the children, however, this situation was not unreasonable. An age difference of 35 years between parent and child suggests that, had circumstances been different, the adoptive mother might have had the child by natural means. The only difference – albeit a large one – is that the early years are missing from their shared experience.

Cultural needs

As previously reported, 65 per cent of the children in the adoptive sample were of white European origin and the others were classified as "black". These black children included ten of African or African-Caribbean origin and seven of mixed parentage. Most had been born in this country.

Out of the 17 black children in the study, one girl of mixed parentage was not placed in her adoptive family for cultural reasons but because she was already known to the white carer through family connections and had a good relationship with her. Later, because this was now regarded as a culturally appropriate placement, the same carer adopted a child of mixed parentage with Down's Syndrome. These cases were an exception to the general rule, however, since all the agencies followed a policy of placing black children (including those of mixed parentage) with people of a similar ethnic and cultural background wherever possible.

In referrals, the need for a black adoptive parent to care for a black child usually ranked as a special need, and when this need was seen to exist it was prioritised. It goes without saying, however, that being black is not a "problem" in the same sense in which physical disability and learning difficulties are problems (although it may involve some social disability), and children placed for adoption for cultural reasons often seemed to benefit from this positive orientation to the referral. The prioritisation of racial or cultural matching also seemed to favour the choice of a single parent in some cases, partly because a black person of single status was seen as preferable to a white couple (although not necessarily preferable to a black couple) and partly, perhaps, because the single black applicant was seen by adoption panels as having a high level of acceptability within the black community. Not without reason, it was assumed that a mother who resembled the child at least partly in heritage and skin colour would be able to provide the child with a strong sense of ethnic identity, and that a mother who had herself grown up as a black person in a white society would be able to help the child with problems of negative discrimination (Ahmed *et al*, 1986; Dickerson, 1995; Dwivedi and Varma, 1996). However, it should be emphasised that the adoptions we studied were shaped by the "same-race" policies of the agencies, and therefore we have no reliable evidence on transracial adoption (Gill and Jackson, 1983; Tizard and Phoenix, 1993; Gaber and Aldridge, 1994).

The black children were generally younger at placement than the white children and had fewer emotional or physical difficulties. These factors also influenced the selection of new carers and the likely success of the adoptions.

Health needs
Whether or not it was a major reason for the type of placement, many of the children in the study had special health needs. At the stage of referral for adoption, children were described as suffering from a variety of conditions which included epilepsy, febrile convulsions, chronic infections (especially of the chest and ears), eczema, asthma and food

allergies. One child was blind. Impaired hearing and speech were common. So were minor physical disabilities. One child could not talk properly because she was tongue-tied; another needed special boots for walking. Twenty-three children out of the total of 48 (almost half the sample) were reported to have learning difficulties. As previously mentioned, nine children had Down's Syndrome, and two of these Down's Syndrome children were also autistic.

All of these conditions required what might be described as "special treatment". The needs were well documented and it may be significant that many of the single people who adopted disabled children had a professional background in nursing, teaching or social work which gave them a good understanding of such children's difficulties. The problems which parents found most troublesome, however, in spite of relevant professional experience in many cases, were emotional and behavioural difficulties. Among children who were referred for adoption after spending several years in the care system, these difficulties were so frequently found as to be almost endemic. The original reasons for accommodating children away from their birth families had included physical and sexual abuse as well as neglect and emotional deprivation. The damage done to the children by many of these experiences was acute, and in some cases it was compounded by frequent changes of home and school and frequent moves between foster carers and residential homes.

Regrettably, the details of the children's previous experience were not always known to the adopters at the time when the "linking" was done.

Table 10
Proven abuse in the children's backgrounds

Type of abuse	No. of boys affected	No. of girls affected	Total no. of children who are known to have suffered this abuse
Physical	1	2	3
Sexual	–	9	9
Physical and sexual	3	3	6
Emotional abuse	1	–	1
Totals	5	14	19

Some children remained relatively silent, but others talked of their previous experiences, including abuse, when they became more trusting and confident in the placement.

For six of the 15 sexually abused children, counselling had been arranged or was already in progress at the time when our interviews were conducted. For another three of these children professional help was planned at a later date. Two had been given counselling or therapy while in the care system, while the remaining four were considered not to need treatment. It was particularly noticeable, however, that no special help had been offered for physical or emotional abuse, regardless of severity. The adoption itself was seen as a way of resolving these problems, and sexual abuse was the only prior experience which appeared to justify special treatment.

The initial introductions

Once a possible link had been agreed, arrangements were made for the prospective parent to meet and get to know the child. This first contact was eagerly awaited, although several parents and children reported that they had felt extremely nervous. Most introductions of children and adopters were carried out in foster homes or residential homes with a fair degree of formality – perhaps in an attempt to defuse the situation of some of its powerful emotional content. The older the child, the greater the degree of anxiety.

During the introduction the single parents were usually seated. The children, if they were over the age of four or five, were encouraged to enter the room and join them. One suspects that this arrangement was made to make the child feel at ease, by lessening the height and size of the adult and giving the child freedom of movement with ready access to the door. Nevertheless some single adoptive parents felt a considerable increase in anxiety as a result of sitting in a room and waiting, and the child was not necessarily reassured to find the adopter already ensconsed in the armchair. One adolescent child said that he had not been told who this person was, and he worried that he was being given yet another social worker.

Two highly successful introductions were organised in a different way. In one case the child (a nine-year-old girl) stood beside her social worker at an upstairs window in the residential home and watched the prospective adopter making her way from the car park. She descended the stairs just as her future mother was entering the hall. Both the adopter and the child agreed in their interviews that this had been a good experience. In the other case a six-year-old girl opened the front door of the foster home and greeted her new mother as she was coming up the path. The parent's recollection was that 'it was wonderful; there was something instant there – a feeling of warmth and spontaneity'. When the girl was interviewed she agreed that she had liked her new mother at first sight. She also indicated that the foster mother had prepared her well for adoption and that this had made the whole process easier

> *She told me adoption is normal, so there's no need to be frightened. It's actually quite exciting.*

In a few cases the parent claimed to have been strongly attracted to the child from the first moment of seeing her photograph and reading the details. A black woman who adopted an 11-month-old girl said that she had felt 'an immediate bond just looking at the picture'. She had a similarly good experience at the first meeting. She had hoped for a small black girl who was energetic and adventurous, and when she first paid a visit to the foster carer's house she was delighted to find that the child was just as she had anticipated:

> *She was rushing around. She was tiny, minuscule – but she could walk and run and go up and down stairs. I couldn't believe it! She was a baby, but on legs! As soon as I saw her, I thought 'Yes'.*

A sense of emotional well-being at the first meeting was always a good start to the relationship even if it was not strictly essential. It seemed to justify careful thought and planning.

Second and subsequent encounters

For much of the introductory period, the prospective adopters and their children were negotiating the basis of their future relationship. The would-be parents felt that they wanted to gain the children's trust, loyalty and affection, and they also needed to gain control. Usually these things went together.

Control was an issue in two senses. Firstly, some of the children were difficult to manage, and there was an expectation that difficult or antisocial behaviour would be controlled by means of the adoption. Secondly, the desire for autonomy in parenting was one of the factors which had propelled single applicants in the direction of adoption rather than fostering or some other form of child care. Because they were keen to establish both control of the child and autonomy in parenting, the prospective adopters had to negotiate with children on the one hand and with the local authority on the other.

The first interactions with the child were often simplified by the fact that there was only one person who was being introduced as a parent; and yet at the same time the feelings of the participants could be quite intense. Everyone else including the supportive social worker could become an outsider who watched from afar. The feeling of exclusivity was heightened by the new parents' ready assumption of responsibility. They responded well to being put in charge of the physical care of young children in foster homes, for example, when they were allocated tasks such as the giving or sharing of food or drink. The child's social worker, who was usually also a woman, had the sense and tact to keep a low profile and to boost the new mother's self-esteem.

One adopter reported an early visit to McDonald's with a ten-year-old child and the child's social worker. While they were eating and drinking, her future daughter started to blow bubbles into a milk shake and showered her with chocolate. The parent's response was risky, but straightforward and direct:

> I said: 'If you do that again I'll put the straw in the bin.' I said it ever so quietly; I just didn't want chocolate all over me. There was the social worker sitting there horrified, thinking: 'She can't do that on her first trip out!' But Marie [the child] responded to it perfectly. She put the lid back on, and finished it off, and held my hand as we went out.

A mixture of affection and firmness on the part of the new parent, together with a sense of pleasure at the meeting, often set the tone for a really good adoption. At the same time children who needed the opportunity to enjoy the close and undivided attention of one permanently caring adult began to relish the experience of relating to the adopter, and they throve on it.

Summary

- All the children placed with the single adopters had special needs. Out of the 48 children who were placed in new families, 22 were older white children, many of whom had a background of abuse and neglect. Of the others, 16 were black children or children of mixed parentage who were deemed to need a culturally specific placement. The remaining ten were physically or mentally disabled.
- The average age at placement for children of all types was between four and five years, but there was a great deal of variation. The black children and the disabled children were the youngest at the time of placement, some of them having been placed for adoption soon after birth. The mentally disabled children had been in their placements for the longest time when the research interviews were held.
- All the agencies followed a policy of placing black children (including those of mixed parentage) with people of a similar ethnic background wherever possible. This seemed to favour the choice of a single parent in some cases.
- Many children had special health needs, and 23 children out of the total of 48 (almost half the sample) had learning difficulties. The adopters were sympathetic to the children's problems and they were often strongly attracted to them at first sight.
- The first introductions were simplified by the fact that only one adult was being introduced to the child, but the adopters and children were often very nervous. Careful planning and structuring of the first meeting was necessary.

9 Post-placement child care

The period of formal introductions, during which the prospective parent and the child met and spent increasing amounts of time together, was reported as a time of jubilation mixed with some stress and anxiety. The child's move into the household was regarded as another major step. One adopter who was an experienced teacher said:

> *Nothing prepares you for the actual experience of looking after a needy child for 24 hours a day.*

However careful the preparations had been, expectations which were based on a knowledge of the child's age and ability sometimes had to be thrown out of the window. Some children regressed when they entered the new family and behaved as if they were much younger than their chronological age. They expected to be carried or to sit on the adopter's lap and be cuddled. They became anxious or tearful when separated from the parent. There was often a temporary increase in bed-wetting or other behaviour which was clearly related to anxiety, and in a few cases there was very disturbed behaviour which resulted in violent aggression against the caring adult. In the aftermath of the placement one woman said that she had found it difficult to sleep at nights, because her pre-adolescent daughter had threatened her with a knife.

However, there were differences depending on the age and vulnerability of the children, and the adopters also had different experiences depending on whether they were novices, old hands or professionals.

The experiences of the "novices"
The people who did not have specific child care or parenting experience were generally younger than the others and, as previously mentioned, four out of seven of these adopters were black. They were appreciative of the fact that they had been to some extent protected by the agency, inasmuch as they had not been given particularly difficult children. Four

of the children adopted by members of this group were young children with cultural needs, and another four white children had some minor emotional problems combined in two cases with mild learning difficulties. In another two cases the adopter was either a blood relative (an aunt) or someone who was already looking after the child.

The young black adopters were also protected in other ways. One woman was helped to find a better council flat, which she badly needed. At the time of our interviews another was being supported through difficult legal proceedings because she hoped to adopt the older sister of a young girl who had recently been placed with her, but quite unexpectedly the child's father had decided to contest the plans for adoption and applied to keep his elder daughter himself. The court had apparently decided that both the single adopter and the child's natural father should be assessed in parallel, and the agency was taking action to prevent the prospective adopter from being humiliated by public assessment in the courts.

Many of the adopters' actual day-to-day activities, in the early stages, were aimed at developing a stable routine for young children. If the child did not have a dietary disorder their concerns moved quickly away from the choice of food and drink, which had been a focus for activity in the pre-placement period, and they started to worry more about bedtime strategies to combat wakefulness and nightmares. The parents, too, had needs which were deserving of respect. In the aftermath of placement, major decisions had to be made about where the children would sleep. One black adopter of a three-year-old child said:

> *When he first came I was going to put him in his own bedroom, and I thought 'No' because at the foster carers' he had the cot near her. So I decided to continue with that for a little while.*

Another who employed a different strategy with her two-year-old daughter said:

> *I had her in my room to start with, but she kept calling me every hour, on the hour. When I had a bad cold I woke up feeling like a zombie. I thought 'That's it. You're in your own room from now on!' She didn't seem to mind.*

Another woman who had been warned to expect sleeping difficulties in the aftermath of her four-year-old child's placement was surprised and pleased when they did not occur. This pattern of anticipating problems which did not materialise was fairly common, and it applied not simply to the management of bedtimes but to other areas of child care. One adoptive parent said that her social worker had warned her about a possible delayed reaction when children are placed.

All the way along the line, I was waiting for something, but no – touch wood – it never happened.

The warnings were valued, however, and the placement experience proved more enjoyable if it was better than expected.

Punitive methods of control can of course lead to escalating over-chastisement, and this was a potential problem for some of the adopters, as it can be for natural parents, when the children presented "challenging behaviour". When their children were disruptive, the inexperienced parents coped best when they set boundaries in a gentle, consistent way which seemed natural to them, but one "novice" adopter said that she had been helped at some stage after the adoption when she chose to train as a foster carer. This training gave her a greater understanding of the experience of children in the care system, and it alerted her to the fact that certain punishments (such as smacking or confinement to a room) might be experienced as abusive. She soon learned to use less threatening and less rejecting methods of control.

Simple behaviourist techniques were widely used in disciplining children and found to be effective. However, the inexperienced adopters who most readily established a good rapport with their children worked from a reward base rather than a punishment base and wherever possible they tended to treat problems as *contextual*. In other words, they saw the features of the situation or the child's environment which were exacerbating the problem and took action to set matters right. One great value of this approach, acknowledged by the adopters who used it, was that it removed some of the pressure of blame from the child and made it possible for changes to be accomplished without loss of face. In relation to the child's past as well as present experiences, the ability to see problems as contextual stated the parent's confidence in the child and held out the promise of a new start. It also created opportunities for appreciating and admiring the positives in the children's behaviour.

Not all of the children adopted by the "novices" were young and problem free. Two of the white parents in this group received, and later adopted, a total of three children who were aged nine, ten and 11 at placement. These children had more problems than the younger adoptees and caused their new parents more anxiety, because of the late transfer to the adoptive home and the background of deprivation and disruption which they had experienced. Two of the children revealed that they had been physically or sexually abused in care. For people without specific child care experience, these disclosures could be especially difficult to cope with. However, the adoptive parents responded with sympathy and concern and sought outside help when it seemed to be required.

The positive, interested and exploring attitudes we have noted here were shared by many of the single adopters, including those who had professional experience, but for the novices these attitudes were essential. They had fewer resources to cope if the relationship swung into negative mode. At the same time the ability to take a refreshingly different view of children's problems was particularly available to some of the "novices", because of their lack of preconceived ideas and the absence of a clinical or pathological approach. One such adopter said of her hyperactive teenage daughter:

She's wonderful and I think, given everything that's happened to her, we can learn a lot from her. Anyone else would have perhaps gone under and been a completely introverted person. She's still willing to get up and try something new. She's very brave, I think.

Similarly one of the male adopters was prepared to cope with some awkward behaviour in order to have a lively son. Referring to his wishes at the time of placement, he said:

I wasn't really "babified". I just wanted a child that was basically full of beans. I didn't want somebody that would sit in a corner reading a book. The foster placement he had was too ingoing.

At the age of five, the child mentioned above had been moved several times within the care system and was already beginning to show signs of being "beyond control"; but he settled happily into the warm and boisterous atmosphere of his adoptive home. His adoptive father provided firm boundaries and successfully treated the previous problems as contextual.

A quieter atmosphere was provided by many of the single women who had applied to adopt. They had risked being stereotyped as "spinsters" and in a few cases discipline was difficult to establish, but children who had lacked one-to-one attention or consistent affection proved that they were capable of making an attachment to these warm-hearted single women and enjoyed living with them.

One 11-year-old boy told us with great pride that his bedroom was 'the biggest room in the house'. When he arrived, he had been feeling very small. His adoptive mother said that he had wanted wallpaper with a childish motif, but he was hesitant about choosing it. She had told him not to worry. 'If you want to change it after a year we can do that; it's only wallpaper.' When they went to choose the carpet, however, it was a different story, and her account of their shopping trip shows how a simple experience such as this could transmit messages of permanence to a child with a background of institutional care.

> I said, 'Remember that you're choosing this carpet for you to live with, for the next three or four or five years. It might even last until you're 17.' I could feel him sort of glowing beside me at the thought of living here with me and this carpet, this year, next year and the years after that.

The experiences of the "old hands"

The seven adopters who had already borne children of their own were less preoccupied with everyday routines, which were generally established quickly without fuss or ceremony. The children who were placed with them included three with Down's Syndrome, four with cultural needs and five with emotional/behavioural difficulties.

These adopters were very aware of the differences between present and past experiences. Mostly the differences were observed with tolerance and interest. For example, one woman – one of the "old hands" who adopted a disabled baby after bringing up her own children – said how strange it was to have charge of a baby whom she had never seen naked, although she had seen him frequently during formal visits to the foster home.

> *The day I brought him home – I was his mother – but I'd never seen him with nothing on! I'd only seen his face.*

If the adoption had been more recent, the foster mother would probably have given her more opportunity to handle the child at an earlier stage. However, the foster carer may have been a little reluctant to hand the baby over to an older woman who was not only single but divorced. Another adoptive mother in this group – a divorced woman who had also adopted an infant with Down's Syndrome – reported that the foster carer would not allow her to touch the baby in her presence, and that she consistently refused to call him by his new name. The foster carers' attitudes were important in the transition to the new placement. Once the adoptive mother was able to take the baby home, however, it did not take long for her to throw off any feeling of strangeness.

> *He was ours as soon as we brought him in. He was a scrawny little thing, but he just belonged as soon as he came.*

The "old hands" were keen to take the children home and absorb them into their families. They did not readily seek social work help, and on the whole they were not well disposed to maintaining contact with the birth family. (This was a problem for all adopters, but especially for the "old hands".) Three of them had resident children of their own at the time when the placement was made, but the age gap was never less than seven years and the new child was apparently well received by the older siblings.

Some adopters felt that they had probably been selected at least partly because of their practical child care experience. However, the relevance of much of their previous experience could be questioned in view of the fact that they were adopting children with special needs, and in fact the adopters themselves were cautious about extrapolating from it. One adopter said that she had profited most from her experiences as a teenager, when she had first become acquainted with needy children.

> *I got quite a good relationship with this Down's girl . . . You don't*

*just keep seeing them as Down's – you see them as people. You see
their personalities and individuality.*

Earlier in life she had also mixed with children who had "emotional and
behavioural difficulties".

*For a long time I was involved with a youth camp, and you get
some really stroppy kids there . . . You discover that it's possible
to build a relationship even with stroppy kids.*

Was it helpful for the adopters to have had their own children? Certainly,
yes. The accounts of the "old hands" suggest that many of the skills they
had acquired were indeed transferable, and they particularly valued the
learned skills of child management. (Confidence was probably a
contributory factor here, and confidence was equally the product of
experience.) One adopter said:

*It's no use being sentimental over children. You have to know when
and how to put your foot down.*

What this response lacked in specificity it made up for in consistency. It
seemed to be particularly valuable for insecure children who had drifted
from one placement to another and who needed the parent to be
predictable at all times.

However, there were other advantages connected with the experience
of having children. The first was the emotional "space" for a dependent
child which had been formed in many households, and which could
usefully be filled by an adoptee when natural children departed. In the
families of "novices" and "professionals", the children sometimes had
to negotiate this space. The second was a resource which was readily
available for the adopter and for the adoptee as well; it was the support
and practical assistance which older children were capable of providing
– especially when these young people were adult or on the verge of
adulthood and did not pose a threat to the adopted child. The third was
an attitude of mind; it was the extra tolerance which long-term
experience of child-rearing had induced – an attitude which was
accentuated, perhaps, by the slowing-down process associated with
ageing. (As one adopter said, 'Time has rounded off the corners'.) This

factor achieves a special importance when we reflect that one proven source of dissatisfaction in adoption is the pressure to fulfil unrealistic parental ambitions (Triseliotis and Russell, 1984).

The fourth advantage possessed in good measure by the "old hands" was an amenable life-style. Women who had organised their domestic and working lives to suit the needs of existing children had few problems in adjusting to fresh demands of a similar nature, because they were accustomed to holding back or even sacrificing their own interests where this appeared to be necessary. They were also accustomed to living on modest incomes. In the adoptive placement their chief satisfaction came, as it had always done, from parenting.

As might be expected, the adopters in this group were slightly older than their counterparts who had no child-rearing experience. The average age of the "novices" at the time of the adoptive placement was 35, and in the case of the "professionals" it was 39. However, the average age of the "old hands" at the time of placement was 41. Once again there was a difference between the experiences of the black and the white adopters, and the average age is lower than it might have been because two out of the three black adopters in this group were in their 30s. One of the placements made with a black adopter and three of those which were made with white adopters involved women in their late 40s, and these women are now in their 50s.

Previous research has identified either old or young age as a risk factor in the approval of adoptive parents. It was certainly true that some problems which were common to all the adoptions (such as stress caused by unruly behaviour on the part of teenage children) were experienced more acutely by older women, and especially by those who were over the age of 45 at the time of the first placement. On the other hand the attempt which had apparently been made to preserve the age gap between adoptive parent and child, so that this gap was between 25 and 35 years on average, automatically meant that older women were matched with older children, some of whom were reckoned to be particularly "hard to place". One woman in her 40s received a girl who at the age of 12 had been classified as unadoptable, after several broken placements, and it is hardly surprising to find that her initial experience was as follows:

She came in here like Lady Muck; this wasn't right, that wasn't right. The home wasn't really good enough for her. She wanted the bedroom rearranged and the bed was too small. She had this way of treating you like you were dirt under her fingernails... Sometimes I felt the problems weren't going to get solved. It was a question of just holding on, at times.

Another factor to be taken into account in any evaluation of the placements is that because some of the adoptions by widows and divorcees took place several years ago (before it was customary to approve women who had always been single), the children adopted by the "old hands" as babies or young children had reached adolescence by the time our interviews were conducted, and a greater volume of potentially problem-ridden material was available for scrutiny. Also, some adoptive mothers had been out of touch with the adoption agency for several years and their support came only from the family and community. In view of this, the older mothers deserve more credit for positive achievements.

Children clearly benefited from the stability which these placements offered, but in a few cases the older adopters themselves might have benefited from a greater degree of official support. At the time of our interviews one woman was struggling with the demands of a new partnership. Another was concerned about isolated incidents of stealing on the part of her adolescent son. Children with mental impairment had been helped by good medical or educational services and strong community networks, but even so, there were hints that some long-standing adopters had few people to talk to about the emotional strains of parenting, or the effect of facing independence in a disabled child who had constantly rewarded the parent simply by being so dependent. One woman who had adopted a child with Down's Syndrome said:

They are babies for longer. Mine is ten years old and I have to do his teeth every morning. If he goes to the toilet he calls me. With a normal child you stop doing that when they're about four or five. I have to do everything for him, all the time.

The mother who made this statement described her adopted son as 'the centre of my life'. She had several adult children, and she had also given birth to a child with Down's Syndrome who died, tragically, a short time before she made the application to adopt. She recognised that the adopted child was in no way a replacement for the one she had lost. As a single parent, she had become accustomed to phrasing her needs in practical terms.

> *What I have always needed is someone to decorate and put doors back on, to fix the hinges and cupboards that are falling off. That's the kind of help I need. I do it all myself.*

At the same time she recounted an incident which had happened shortly before our interview, on a day in December. She said that she had passed a Christmas tree in the market place and paid (as was requested by a local charity) to hang a bauble on the tree with the name of a person on it. She had written the name of the child who died 11 years ago, and then she had stood quietly in the rain and wept.

The experiences of the "professionals"

Single people with professional backgrounds were allocated most of the children in the sample who might be regarded as seriously "hard-to-place". Between them, the 16 people in this group adopted or had plans to adopt 28 children. Seven of the children were mentally or physically disabled, eight had cultural needs, and 13 had emotional or behavioural difficulties.

Like all the other adoptive applicants, those who had professional experience had applied to the adoption agencies because they wanted to care for children and young people in a parenting role. They had high standards and were sometimes anxious. They wanted to be good mothers or fathers, but they also felt that their acquired skills were valuable, and this feeling contributed not only to the maintenance of their self-esteem but to the actual success of the adoptions. Another helpful feature was that – with only a few exceptions – they related easily to the social workers in the adoption agencies. They had generally enjoyed the approval process. Habits of interdisciplinary working, combined with similar backgrounds and common interests, had created a common culture of which they were a part.

One of the single adopters – a specialist teacher of deaf and blind children – first met her severely disabled son in a professional context. When she realised that adoption was a possibility she felt able to approach the child's social worker and discuss the situation. However, this woman quite correctly recommended that she should seek help elsewhere since, as social worker for the child, she 'might have to hand him over to different adoptive parents'. Far from feeling put down by this advice, the adopter appreciated the reasons for it and she went on to form a good relationship with the agency worker who helped her through the approval process.

Many prospective adopters would have felt daunted by the problems of the disabled child referred to above. Although he was aged four at the time of his placement he had no language, sight or hearing. At the time of the research he was aged 14, and seemed to have made quite remarkable progress during the last ten years. His blindness had remained, but his deafness proved to be the result of neglected glue ear, and after this was rectified he started to talk. He was referred to as 'a chatterbox'. At the age of four he was failing to thrive and he was the size of a one-year-old. At age 14 he was 5'6" tall and growing fast.

In addition to his physical difficulties, this deaf and blind child was severely traumatised at the time of his placement as a result of being verbally and physically abused in a variety of settings (he had been moved ten times). He had a great fear of being hurt or moved elsewhere, and he tended to sit on the floor and circle aimlessly. Until the age of seven he had to have someone from home to stay with him in school, yet his present head teacher does not identify him as a child with any emotional disturbance.

How have these successes been achieved? According to the adopter, the key factor has been the slow and steady development of a one-to-one relationship, based on shared understanding and sympathy. As an alternative to strong discipline, plans and patterns of behaviour have been "negotiated". An atmosphere of care and respect, together with affection, has enabled her son to develop into 'a sociable, trusting person' who is fun to be with: 'The older he gets, the more fun he becomes.' At the same time she is in touch with her own feelings, and knows 'what it is like to be tired and fed up as well as pleased'.

Another white woman who worked as a health visitor received a seven-year-old girl who had been sexually abused. As she got to know the child, she found that in this badly mistreated girl there was a distressing absence of the ability to recognise and express feeling. The child seemed tense and rigid and did not eat properly. Refusing to write off these difficulties as "teething problems", she approached the situation through the skills which she felt she had learnt as a health visitor.

> *I taught her again how to smell and taste and touch – the way you do with little children, putting their hands in the feely box and saying, 'What's this?'. I taught her how to eat and swallow – to smell first and feel with the lips, then taste in the mouth, and feel it going down to give a sensation in the stomach. After six months she was able to feel her tummy.*

In stark contrast to this, a black health visitor reported that the two boys she had adopted between the ages of four and six were 'not greatly damaged' and it seemed as though they had always been there.

Only four of the 16 professionally qualified adopters were black women. This situation probably reflects social and educational opportunities rather than the selection of women for adoptive parenting, but it reminds us that it is misleading to equate the experiences of the black adopters with those of their white counterparts simply on the grounds that they share unmarried status or a common occupational grading.

When asked about the advantages or disadvantages of professional skills or knowledge in her experience of adoption, the black health visitor said:

> *Being a professional prepared me for the intrusion of social services. It would have been harder for me if I hadn't known how they work, and if I hadn't known about the structure of health and social services. I ask questions like that as well when I visit people … It's easier for me to understand the intrusion because of the work I do.*

These very different accounts indicate how the previous experience of the adopters contributed to the children's post-placement experience in diverse and sometimes unexpected ways. Sometimes special skills seemed to be required, but in the actual day-to-day work of caring, the professional adopters were drawing on their moral values, their capacity for affection or altruism, their experiences of family living and their understanding of relationships in general. In this respect they made common cause with the novices and the old hands.

Summary

- The child's transition to the adopter's household was not always smooth, and various difficulties were experienced during the "settling-in period". Sometimes the children regressed and became withdrawn or tearful. At other times they presented challenging behaviour. Even threats of violence were not unknown.

- The inexperienced adopters whom we have termed "novices" were given a lot of protection by the agency. This was done through careful selection of the children who were placed with them and through the provision of support for legal proceedings, etc. One of their main resources, apart from energy and commitment, was a positive attitude to the children. They succeeded best when they worked from a reward base rather than a punishment base, and when they treated problems as contextual.

- At the time of the research many of the "old hands" who had brought up their own children to adulthood were caring for adolescents, some of whom had been adopted several years ago. They were sometimes struggling with intractable problems, but they had other life experiences which were relevant in addition to the experience of bringing up their own children.

- Some of the single people with current or previous professional experience had adopted children with severe difficulties. Whether or not they drew extensively on their professional experience as a knowledge base, it gave them confidence and understanding of services. Sometimes exceptional results were achieved.

- Regardless of whether or not they had worked professionally in one of the caring services, the adopters recognised that they were in a family situation. After the placement they drew heavily on their own experience of family living.

10 Employment and finances

A major issue to be faced by some single adopters was whether or not their employment could continue in some form after the placement, and if not, how it could be replaced.

The accounts of recent placements are valuable because significant changes often seemed to happen in the early stages, and especially in the first few months after the child entered the household. Nevertheless these accounts are usefully brought into perspective by being placed alongside those of long-standing adopters, many of whom started caring for children in a very different social context. More of the widows and divorcees who had previously looked after their own children worked in the home environment, while the group of single people approved from 1990 onwards, among whom there was a much larger proportion of the never married, were mostly in permanent jobs.

Adoption allowances

Thirty-five children in the study contributed indirectly to the income of their new families by attracting an adoption allowance. The remaining 13 children did not receive financial help from social services except during the initial placement period. The availability, or otherwise, of an allowance was important because it affected the total resources of the household.

Adoption allowances have had a rather difficult history. Their introduction was given cautious approval in the Adoption Act of 1976, but the schemes proved to be controversial because of the popular feeling that payment of any kind contradicted the basic principles of adoption. However, some monitoring research carried out by the National Children's Bureau in the 1980s demonstrated the importance of adoption allowances in facilitating the adoption of "hard to place" children. The central principle according to which payments are made still does not incorporate any notion of entitlement. It is that:

An adoption allowance may be payable to help secure a suitable adoption where a child cannot be readily adopted because of a financial obstacle. (DoH, 1991).

Given that the adoptions took place at different points in time, there were three factors which together appeared to control the availability and the amount of adoption allowances received by people in the study: firstly, the age of the child, together with the degree of disability or the extent of the child's special needs; secondly, the income level of the prospective parent; and thirdly, the length of time which had elapsed since the placement. Some of the older adoptions were not subsidised, although funds might have been made available today.

When an allowance was not given, the parent had often not asked for it. In one case the parent did not appear to know that she might have been eligible, but this was unusual since most adopters knew that the provision for allowances existed, and some chose not to apply.

When adoption allowances were awarded, the actual amount varied considerably from one authority to the next. One mother of several children complained that she received as much for one child who was badly disabled as she did for another who had 'virtually no problems at all'. Local authorities in industrial areas, she said, were more generous in their allocation of funds.

If you get a child from somewhere quite posh, you're expected to do it for love.

Generally speaking an allowance of between £30 and £75 a week seemed to be offered when a young child with special needs was in a recent placement. (Some of these were fostering allowances, since the adoption had not always been completed by the time our research was conducted.) Between £75 and £150 a week was received by the adoptive parents of older children with special needs, but particularly difficult adolescents might attract allowances of between £150 and £200. The maximum amount paid for one child in the study was £216 a week. This was described as a "triple allowance" paid to one adoptive mother who was caring for an exceptionally hard-to-place teenager. She had no other resources except income support.

The slightly lower allowances given to children who had been in their placements for a long time did not always reflect a low starting rate. In some cases an inadequate system of review appeared to have held back the updating of the allowance. It was not unusual to find that responsibility had been placed on the adoptive parent to initiate a review if he or she felt that one was required, and although the local authority had also retained the power to initiate reviews, some parents felt that this would happen only if it was in the interests of the authority to do so (that is, because the parent's income had increased and the allowance might conceivably be reduced). The Adoption Allowance Regulations state that reviews should be held annually, in addition to responding to changes in circumstances. Nevertheless the picture resembles "gate-keeping" rather than "enabling".

Local authority resources are limited, but it should be noted that in almost all cases in the study, the parents reported that the financial cost of raising the children was much greater than they had anticipated. In part, this was due to the high cost of substitute child care, but it was also due to the exceptional needs of the children who had been adopted. If the children were dyslexic or had learning difficulties, parents sometimes paid for private tutors to help them to catch up. If they had physical difficulties, such as poor co-ordination, money was found for activities such as swimming, gymnastics or dancing. Clothes, shoes and property wore out quickly when the children were hyperactive, and young black children who had been placed for adoption mainly for social and cultural reasons required expenditure on air fares if they were to be kept in touch with relatives overseas.

Parents who did not receive financial help paid for all expenditure out of their own salaries, apart from the addition of child benefit, and recognised (usually without rancour) that they were considerably worse off as a result. Those who received an adoption allowance, on the other hand, said that it was just enough to enable them to preserve the equilibrium.

Combining paid work and child care

At the time of our study ten of the adopters (one-third of the sample) were unemployed. The other adopters were all doing paid work on a regular basis either full-time or part-time, and they had devised ways of fitting their employment round child care arrangements.

Table 11 gives the employment status of the adopters at the time of the interviews. The changing patterns of employment in the immediate post-placement period, and the breakdown of numbers in each category, are reported in Table 12. These figures give no indication of the skill and ingenuity with which people constructed individual strategies to meet both their own and their children's needs.

Table 11
Employment status of the adopters

Employment status	No. of adopters	Per cent
Working full-time	13	44
Working part-time	7	23
Unemployed	10	33
Total	30	100

Table 12
Adopters' employment patterns in the first six months following placement of a child

Employment pattern	No. of adopters
Continued working as before	10
Made minor changes or reduced number of hours	8
Changed type of employment	5
Found employment as a result of the adoption	2
Remained unemployed	3
Gave up work	2
Total	30

Many parents had deliberately applied for a child of school age, or at least nursery school age, so that they could continue working, and this is reflected in the fact that within six months of the placement 25 out of the 30 adopters (83 per cent of the adult sample) were in full or part-time employment. There was also a considerable degree of stability in people's employment patterns. At the time of the research 18 of the 25 working parents were still in the same jobs, or at least in the same type of work which they had previously undertaken, but many of these people had made subtle modifications to their working lives.

Continuing work as before
Parents who continued to work in the same way, in the same occupation and with the same number of hours as before, belonged mainly to Category 2 of the Registrar General's classification of employment categories. That is, they ranked as "lower professionals". Nine out of ten of these parents were women, and four of the women were black. Mostly, they worked full-time. They were all in their 30s or early 40s at the time of the first placement, and with only two exceptions they adopted school-aged children. They were outgoing, determined and energetic.

The full-time workers in this group consisted of two teachers, two health visitors, one nursery proprietor, one garage owner, one cancer nurse, one businesswoman and a university lecturer. All of them had time off for the initial placement and then resumed work at the same level. By means of a mixture of formal and informal supports, they had reliable and sometimes complex arrangements for child care.

The odd one out in this predominantly business and professional group is a woman who was employed part-time as a social services home help. She had two adopted children and received allowances for both of them, which enabled her to pay for childminding. However, her situation becomes more understandable when we realise that the common factors that enabled people to continue working were autonomy, freedom to plan the work on a case-by-case or unit-by-unit basis, good colleague support and the availability of stand-ins for routine tasks. These adopters also seemed to have a degree of responsibility which was not unduly burdensome, and they had the power to seek help in an emergency without totally disrupting the organisation.

All the people in this group felt that they could pay for child care if it was needed. Most of their leisure time was spent with the children – sometimes in shared activities which were recreational for both.

Making minor changes

Most parents in employment, whether full-time or part-time, were eager to maximise the time spent with the children. Five parents among the full-time workers felt that this could only be achieved by a changed pattern of working. Like the people mentioned above they were in their 30s or early 40s, but they had adopted younger or more demanding children.

The five parents who made minor changes without reducing the number of their working hours were all involved in caring services. Two of the adopters were teachers of children with special needs, one was a principal social worker, one a staff member from a community home and one a health manager. Wherever possible, they shifted the pattern of employment in such a way that their own leisure time coincided with the child's waking hours and non-school time. This gave them more opportunity to share sports or hobbies, to help with problems or tasks such as homework, to converse and generally to set up and enjoy the kind of productive periods of interaction which are often described as "quality time".

One common way in which these adopters increased the amount of time with a school-aged child, while carrying their full share of the employment workload, was to shift tasks from one part of the day to another. For example, they would take time off in order to be at home when the child returned from school, and balance this by taking home work to be completed when the child was in bed. One adopter carried out tasks in a more concentrated way during the day and cut out meetings at anti-social hours. Another exchanged duties with a colleague in order to streamline the pattern of working. In ways like these, the parents made sure that children did not spend more hours than were strictly necessary in substitute care.

Several parents in this group relied heavily on the very adequate help they received from the extended family. Two parents initially tried to work flexibly enough to do without substitute care entirely, but the attempt was not successful. In one case a teacher who had negotiated special working hours for the first six months of the placement found that she was unable to get home at the appointed time because of pressure of work, and consequently there were a few occasions when the child was left unsupervised. She responded to this situation by arranging for a regular childminder. In the other case the employer became unhappy and the parent herself felt that she could not work as productively as before, because her attempt to do three hours' work at home in the evening was foiled by the length of time it took to get through the child's homework. She responded by cutting down her hours.

Reducing the number of hours

A straightforward reduction in working hours may seem an obvious course of action for people who want to continue working when they have young children, but it was an option chosen by surprisingly few parents in the sample. The main reason seems to be that it was seldom available as an option.

As already mentioned, only seven out of the 30 adopters were working part-time when our interviews were conducted, and most of these people were in jobs which had been designated as part-time from the start. This finding highlights the rigidity of the employment situation in which most of the female adopters found themselves. It is of course true that many of them would not have wanted to reduce their working hours because of the loss of income or loss of responsibility which would have been involved, and in the case of well-paid professional people a switch to part-time working in a different field would have meant the sacrifice of skills and a disproportional amount of the adopter's income.

As other studies have pointed out, part-time and full-time jobs are different in kind (Haskey, 1993). There were very few single adopters who worked in the fields frequented by other lone mothers in the population – namely catering, cleaning, hairdressing and other personal service jobs, or selling, or clerical and related occupations. Only one woman in the study (a black woman) regularly undertook casual work in a variety of occupations. She planned her post-placement career just as carefully as full-time workers, and at the time of the placement she exchanged a part-time job as an auxiliary nurse for a part-time job in catering because it offered more flexible working hours.

In all, there were three adopters in the study who successfully cut down their working hours without a change of occupation when a child was placed with them. The first was a white social services manager who was heavily engaged in adoption and fostering work, and who obtained permission to work half-time on the grounds that her experience as an adoptive mother was highly relevant to the employment. The second was a woman, also white, who had been working for the education department of a large London borough. She moved her work-base to a small language and literacy unit, where she began working part-time and then increased to four days a week. Her comments about her employment were as follows:

> *It's very flexible. I'm very lucky, really. I have a very under-standing director. We're all women! Over the period during the adoption I took time off and they were very supportive. There were lots of presents.*

The third adopter in this group was a young black social worker who negotiated part-time working by means of a job share. Like the woman mentioned above, she also transferred her place of employment but she felt that her conditions of work had worsened, and she also suffered financially from the reduction in hours because she received no adoption allowance for one of her adopted children.

Apart from these three people, the adopters who wanted to make substantial alterations to their working hours changed the type of their employment or gave up work altogether.

Changing the type of employment

When the focus of the parents' work was outside the home they some-times encouraged a feeling of integration by taking the adopted children into the workplace. For many of the women who changed their employ-ment, however, this process happened in reverse. From outside employ-ment they moved back into the home, which then *became* the workplace.

Parents who turned to home-based employment after a child was placed with them did so for a number of reasons. Often they wanted freedom to be at home with young children and to plan their own day without sacrificing all their earning capacity, but another major consideration was that they were exchanging a stressful job for one which was less stressful. For example, one adopter exchanged class teaching for individual tuition.

Sometimes the new occupation provided a job which was part-time and at least partly experimental, since adoption itself was a form of innovation which encouraged the adopter to explore new fields. This feeling of "making a new start" could be important – especially to the novice adopters. One adopter who had previously done routine clerical work set up a successful business as an aromatherapist in her front room.

Working in the home environment of course carried with it the risk of social isolation, but the carers we interviewed were seldom at risk of becoming totally isolated since they were providing a service which was used by other people.

In the study as a whole, childminding was a popular choice of occupation since it provided home-based employment with flexible working hours, a modest increase in income and a chance to try out new skills. It also helped the neighbourhood integration of the single adopter. By gaining knowledge of other children and finding out what they could do or enjoy, the new parent felt that she had some yardstick against which to measure her own children's progress, and the experience also provided company (with a necessary amount of adult supervision) for the adopted child.

Altogether five women in the study were involved in childminding or related activities such as nursery work or "link" schemes. The financial gain from home-based employment was often slight, but when disadvantaged children were at risk of being outlawed or discriminated against in the neighbourhood, the parent was happy to work in exchange for social rather than economic benefits. On a more general level we can see that a form of community-based reciprocity was taking place. Some single parents who worked outside the home were in need of substitute care, and some of the single adopters who worked at home were providing it. Financial transactions were a way of regulating this exchange. Most of the adopters did not insist on an accurate balance, however. They were content to give more than they received. Some parents also took part in reciprocal child care arrangements which did not involve money changing hands, but participation in babysitting circles was usually difficult because of the lack of a partner, and single women could only respond to "gifts" of babysitting by looking after the sitter's child during the day. This was a situation which was easily regularised by the parent's becoming a registered childminder, and at the same time it gave the parent the option of returning some favours in kind.

These movements did not of course happen entirely without external pressures. When women changed their employment radically at the time when the placement was made, there was often a feeling of dissatisfaction with a previous job situation which had become stagnant or unrewarding. Whether or not redundancy was on the horizon, some women expressed a wish to abandon boring or highly competitive jobs in favour of employment which was emotionally enriching, and the move towards adoption could be seen as part of this trend. Several adopters were happily engaged, to a greater or lesser extent, in voluntary work.

Remaining unemployed

The adopters who were not in employment at the time of the placement, and who had no intention of re-entering employment, were older mothers who had never worked outside the home apart from taking casual jobs which were temporary or part-time. They belonged to the group we have previously identified as "old hands". Three mothers in particular had devoted most of their time previously to bringing up children, and were happy to continue this pattern.

There was a lot of similarity between the three women. In addition to having children of their own, they had all been divorced or separated at an early stage. They therefore had a lot of experience of single parenthood. Each of them had also adopted a Down's Syndrome child, at least in the first instance. (One had gone on to adopt two other children.) They had firm and sometimes rigid views on child upbringing, but they had considerable practical and caring skills and they were totally devoted to their task. Their main satisfaction in life came from caring for dependent children.

One of the women in this group was a little wistful when thinking about unfulfilled ambitions, and she particularly regretted her lack of education. However, on the whole these mothers were happy with the work that they were doing and felt well regarded by their local communities, in which they were firmly rooted.

Finding employment as a result of the adoption

A small but interesting group of adopters were those who entered or seemed about to enter employment as a result of the adoption. They were women who had given up work or had previously been unemployed, although they had often been involved in the care of dependent relatives. Through their experience of the adoption approval process, and particularly as a result of their contact with social workers, they began to see that they had in fact been under-achieving and had under-valued their own practical and intellectual skills.

The two adopters in this group who made real progress in finding employment were both poor black women, and the catalyst in each case was a sympathetic social worker (herself a black woman) who acted as a role model. One of the women became a short-term foster carer and learnt to take part in assessments on behalf of the local authority. Another became a funded student on an access course leading to professional social work. Another black woman who was unemployed at the time of the interview stated her intention of moving into adoption and fostering work as soon as the opportunity became available.

Naturally enough, the agency workers supported these initiatives. At the same time the social workers were reported as showing some anxiety if the adopters seemed to be moving too rapidly towards self-advancement. They probably felt some responsibility for this unexpected change in the situation and worried about protecting the interests of the adopted child.

Giving up work

For most of the adopters who left work after the adoption, the transition to full-time motherhood happened slowly. They continued working for a while, then withdrew from employment when the need arose – usually when more children were adopted.

There were four parents in the study who had adopted three children or more. One was previously unemployed, but the other three left work at the time when the third child was adopted. It seemed that most of the mothers who arrived at this point were abandoning the prospects of paid work at least for the time being. It is not hard to understand the reasons, since it would obviously be difficult for anyone to remain in permanent employment after adopting three or four children with special needs.

When adopting again, some parents began to examine the possibility of adopting sibling groups. They also explored the possibility of a child of a different sex, or a different age, or a different type of disability. The decision to abandon employment gave them more flexibility. One mother said:

> With the fourth child I'd decided I wanted a baby. I was going to give up work – this was the right time to give up work – so therefore I could take a little baby, whereas before I'd not been able to do that.

Financial considerations were important. The third or fourth adoption was also the point at which the provision of allowances usually made it possible for the parent to derive a full-time income without recourse to other sources of help. At the point where allowances matched existing income, it was feasible for parents to choose adoption as an alternative to paid employment without feeling that they were sliding rapidly down the financial scale.

The people in the study who abandoned paid work early were predominantly women in the lower income groups. As a result, they risked being seen as unduly dependent on state benefits. To people who looked at the situation from a different viewpoint, however, they could appear to be exceptionally caring and altruistic. The reality is that their work conditions were generally tighter than those of the managerial or professional adopters, with less room to manoeuvre and sometimes less sympathy available for employees caught up in domestic problems. Lacking power to shift arrangements within the organisation, the single women on low incomes had to leave work to accommodate the needs of their children.

These factors clearly had an influence in shaping people's employment careers and they also affected the women's feelings about the relative desirability of work and home, since both environments were capable of providing benefits for parents and children alike.

Summary
- Seventy-five per cent of the children in the study came to their new

homes with the promise of an adoption allowance. The actual amount varied with the children's age and the extent of their special needs, together with the income or capital of the adopter and the length of time during which the child had been in placement. The lowest amount awarded, for a young black child, was £30 per week. The highest, for a white teenager, was £216.

- At the time of the study ten of the adopters (one-third of the adult sample) were unemployed. The other adopters were doing paid work on a regular basis, either full-time or part-time.

- After the placement, ten adopters continued to work in the same way as before. They were mainly professional and business people with good resources for substitute child care. Five adoptive parents continued in the same employment but with minor changes, and three succeeded in reducing their hours.

- A number of women changed their type of employment so that they could work in the home environment. Child-minding was a popular occupation, not only because it was home-based but because it helped to integrate the adopted child in the neighbourhood. Altogether five women were involved in childminding or related activities such as nursery work or "link" schemes.

- Three black women were helped to find employment through their contact with social workers. One became a short-term foster carer. Another became a funded student on an access course leading to social work, and another intended to move into adoption and fostering work.

- Except in the few cases where the adopters were permanently unemployed, the transition to full-time parenthood happened gradually. For three parents it was timed to coincide with the third adoption. It was at this point that the cumulative supply of adoption allowances made withdrawal from work a real possibility.

11 Family and community relationships

Most of the adopters had close and enduring relationships with at least some members of the extended family. A distinction was always made in the interviews between kinship networks and what Firth calls "effective kin" (Firth, 1970), effective kin being those extended family members with whom people were involved in "an active social relation". Friends were sometimes more important than family because these relationships had been made on the basis of shared interests. Nevertheless for most adopters, longstanding family members continued to be the first port of call in an emergency.

A typical family structure at the start of adoption
The family system represented as a genogram in Figure 1 belongs to a single woman who recently adopted a nine-year-old girl. It is typical of many family structures found in the study, and for this reason we can hazard a guess that it is a pattern preferred by the selecting agencies or one that gives applicants the confidence to proceed. What are the key features? Firstly, it is a multi-generation family. Secondly, the single parent and the adopted child are buttressed by other family members, both older and younger, and surrounded by people of both sexes.

The third feature to note is the importance of the siblings of the adoptive parent and the good supply of cousins for the adopted child. (It should be noted that black children reported more contact with their adoptive cousins than did white children.) The family circle represented here has been extended by the marriage of one person (the adopter's brother) to a divorced woman with children. Like marriage, divorce either adds or subtracts whole clusters of people in these family networks, and in some cases it seems to have increased the adoptive parent's understanding and tolerance of structural changes – a circumstance which helped to ease the relationship between the adoptive family and the child's birth family.

Fourthly, the ages of the various family members are probably significant. This single woman applied to adopt in her early 40s, whereas her siblings had all married and had children at a younger age. Consequently the cousins were all somewhat older than the adoptee. In an ideal situation they would form a group of interested and relatively tolerant playmates, not given to rivalry and not usually diverting the attention of adults from the needs of the adopted child. However, as the adopters were well aware, everything depended on the quality of individual relationships and the extent of interaction between members of the extended family.

Patterns of closeness

In terms of closeness, the actual family system which is depicted in Figure 1 divided up along gender lines. The adoptive mother had a strong bond with her own mother, who was a widow, and her closest sibling was her married sister. (The link between sisters is very common in the study.) Perhaps because the adopted child saw more of these family members than the others, and perhaps because she was a girl, she had a special feeling of closeness with her mother, her grandmother and her aunt.

Figure 1
The genogram of one single adopter and her child

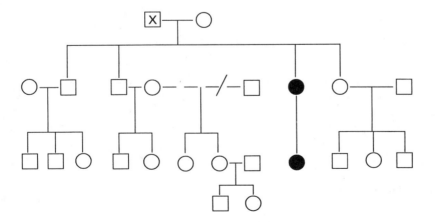

Generally speaking women who had adopted boys made more effort to stay in touch with their brothers, although the need for male role models in mother/son families may have been over-emphasised (Silverstein and Rashbaum, 1995). It is clear that some adopted girls also valued contact with their uncles and grandfathers, although this contact was seen as less necessary at the time of the adoption, and all children benefited by not being confined too rigidly to gender roles.

At the time of our interviews the average number of adoptive family members seen by each child on a weekly basis was three, including the adoptive parent. When extended to include family members seen less than weekly, the average number of relatives with whom the child had contact on a regular basis was between four and five (see Table 13). It does seem as though the majority of single-adopter households were happy and stable when the child had good interactions with at least three close relatives including the adoptive parent, and if this minimum number of relatives was not available, then friendship networks were called upon to make up the difference.

Help received from family and friends

Friends (and also some family members) were not automatically

Table 13
Face-to-face contact within the adoptive family

Relative in the adoptive family	No. of children who see this relative at least weekly N = 48	No. of children who see this relative less than weekly N = 48	Total no. of children who see this relative N = 48
Adoptive parent	48	–	48 (100%)
Grandparent	19	14	33 (69%)
Adopted sibling	31	–	31 (65%)
Non-adopted sibling	8	3	11 (23%)
Uncle or aunt	4	6	10 (21%)
Cousin	4	3	7 (15%)
Mother's cousin	1	–	1
Niece	–	1	1

supportive of the adoptions. Some people were reported to be enthusiastic about the proposal from the start. Others mulled it over and said that they understood the adopter's reasons for applying although they had reservations about the wisdom of the decision – usually because they were protective of the adopter and concerned about what he or she might be "taking on". One adopter was touched and embarrassed because her friends regarded her as a saint. Another common reaction was that people avoided contact because they did not know how to react appropriately, and they needed help to understand.

Fortunately the people who were closest to the adopters usually ended up by being supportive. There is ample evidence, in the study, of the importance of informal networks for each of the groups we have identified – the "novices", the "old hands" and the "professionals". There was also some evidence that the situation changed over time, not because people fell out with each other but because they entered another phase in the life-cycle. About a year after the placement of his nine-year-old son, one adoptive parent reported the change in his circumstances as follows:

> *Friends have always been extremely important to me all my life, and so it continues. What's interesting is that up to now I have tended to see single friends more, but in this situation I tend to see friends with children.*

Another longstanding adopter exchanged visits with a former school-friend when her children were young, but found that her relationship pattern shifted as the children of both families turned into young adults with different interests.

For most of the adopters it was important to have friends with children of a similar age to their own. However, the inter-child relationships could be difficult. People who would have liked to have offered support to the adoptive parent were understandably protective of their own children and ended the acquaintance if the adopted child behaved aggressively towards them. In cases such as these, the adopter needed friendship with other, single colleagues or with adoptive parents who had experienced similar problems.

A view which was expressed more than once – especially by the professional adopters – was that friends who shared their values had more understanding of the situation than family members who were simply related by the blood-tie. Friends were therefore more capable of providing informed advice as well as sympathy, but at the same time the emotional support provided by extended family members and the sense of belonging which their attitudes conveyed were important both to the adopter and to the child. In at least one case the effect of this dichotomy was that the adoptive parent talked more freely about problems to trusted friends and colleagues, and withheld negative information about the child from grandparents or aunts and uncles in order not to endanger these crucial relationships.

What help was most valued?
Whatever the exact balance between friends and family members, the adopters clearly needed people with whom they could share the problems and at least some of the responsibility of bringing up the children. Less obviously, perhaps, they needed to share the good times and the evidence of progress.

The adoptive mother of a young child who was physically disabled and had learning difficulties said:

> *I can remember when Lennie learned to stand up in his cot. I actually came downstairs and phoned my Mum, because there's only my Mum I could tell. I said: 'Guess what? Lennie's stood up in his cot!' She said: 'That's brilliant; but do you know it's five o'clock on a Sunday morning?'.*

The main "input" to the adoption from family members and friends was emotional support. Secondly, the adopters benefited from the provision of practical help such as babysitting or holiday care, and thirdly, the network provided opportunities for children to contribute to the welfare of others. However, it is difficult to conceptualise family relationships according to an input-output model. The main advantages to the child stemmed from his or her membership of the household and community, and in this respect they were part of the adoptive experience itself.

Much of the family's visible input, of course, was concerned with practical help. Where the work patterns of the parent did not necessitate regular child-minding or nursery attendance, assistance with child care was provided in large measure by friends and family members. This help included both babysitting and respite care.

Ten per cent of the children in the adoptive sample lived in households where there was a resident grandparent (three grandmothers and two grandfathers). In 12 other families babysitting was done by the maternal grandmother or by other relatives living close by. Membership of babysitting circles was not usually considered possible because of the difficulty the adoptive parents experienced in returning the service, and sitters who needed payment were rarely engaged in the evenings because of the high cost. As a result, the adopters tended to stay at home in the evenings if there was no informal help available, or else they went out when it was possible for them to be accompanied by their children.

Services such as babysitting were not always prized as highly as conventional married couples might expect. There was no need for regular outings to maintain an adult partnership, and babysitting was often considered less valuable than forms of help which took the child out into the community. One adopter said that she was fortunate in having 'a lot of friends who will take a child out for tea, or to the cinema'. Another woman who had adopted two young black boys said that the children liked to spend an occasional night or a weekend with her sister. Clubs and after-school activities for children were very much valued.

Whether or not they were capable of providing help with child care, grandparents, where they existed, were an important "anchor" for the family. Other relatives including the young adults who were the parents' natural children had specific contributions to make. If they lived nearby and visited the family frequently, they sometimes accompanied younger children on activities too energetic or too demanding for the parent to attempt. For example, Alexander's older sister took her younger adopted siblings on shopping expeditions, and this was appreciated because she understood teenage fashion and had good dress sense.

All these forms of "support" were valued, but a point which needs to be made is that the passage of help between relatives and adopted children was not always one way. Once they were settled in the household the children enjoyed doing things for other people. Ten-year-old Natalie regularly took her partially-sighted grandfather to the Blind Club. She described herself in her interview as 'a helping person', and this was confirmed by her mother's account of their joint visits to the supermarket.

Natalie is brilliant! She unpacks everything at the check-out and I pack it at the other end of the counter. We have got it off to a fine art. We have a great big trolley-full, and it's done in minutes.

Suzanne's adoptive mother spoke of her pleasure at her child's expression of concern when she returned home after an operation.

I was at home here, not feeling very well after surgery, and there was a little child coming into my room to find out if my tummy was all right and if I wanted a glass of water.

Some adopted children reported that they enjoyed entertaining young friends, or playing with a small niece or nephew during visits to the extended family. Fifteen-year-old Martin and 12-year-old Ben talked to their neighbour's children. Eight-year-old William took particular pleasure in teaching two-year-old Thomas to ride a tricycle. The children's delight in these activities showed how much they valued the chance to contribute, instead of being made to feel that they were on the receiving end of the family's charity.

Membership of community groups
Relationships with the community at large could prove much more problematic than those with family and friends – especially if the adopter was not well-known in the community and if the children posed risks to themselves or other people. Professional adopters were more vulnerable in this respect, because their social networks were often widely spaced geographically.

Black children were generally accepted in the multiracial communities where their adoptive parents lived, apart from isolated incidents of racism. The adopters of children with Down's Syndrome also felt valued by their communities, even if the support offered was sometimes patronising and lacking in understanding. (One adopter of several disabled children reported that a man had recently approached her in the street and tried to press money into the children's hands.)

The most serious difficulties in integrating children were experienced when they had previously been abused and neglected, or had suffered a lot of disruption in the care system. Friction was especially likely to occur at the start of placements, when the children reacted to distress by behaving in a way which was regarded as anti-social. One adopter reported that she had moved to a new estate when the child was placed, seeking only a house which she could afford and which had the requisite number of rooms. However, during the next few months her car was kicked by neighbours until it had dents in it, and her child was victimised by other children in the school playground. Another adopter found that her sexually abused child attracted unwelcome attention from local youths. At times such as these, the support of well-informed and trustworthy people was invaluable.

In general the adopters preferred informal social contact to membership of organisations. However, two different kinds of "self-support group" were described favourably by the adults in the study. One was a group of adoptive parents, both married and single. The other was a group of single parents. They were both women's groups. The few women who went to the meetings or organised them in their own homes drew considerable strength from them, but membership of a group of adoptive parents was sought after and valued more highly than membership of a single-parent group.

Parent-link groups arranged by PPIAS (Parent to Parent Information on Adoption Services) were seen as friendly and well organised. Since they formed part of a national network it was possible for adoptive parents to join a new group – or even, as happened in one case, to start one – when they moved to a new area, and they were also kept in touch with other parents' experiences and current debates through the quarterly PPIAS journal, *Adoption UK*. In addition, two parents with a professional orientation were members of British Agencies for Adoption and Fostering (BAAF).

Single-parent groups were valued as a source of fellowship; but they were organised by churches, and this did not suit single adopters who were not religious. For two of those who did believe, they were a great source of support.

One woman who had adopted disabled children joined the Down's Association, but left it when she discovered that she was uncomfortable in a group of mothers who had given birth to disabled children. She had experienced none of their sense of guilt. She felt that the issues she faced were different, and this is one more indication that many of the women in the study defined themselves as *adoptive* parents.

Support from professional agencies
In recent years the problems which may drive adoptive parents to seek help from professional agencies have been increasingly well documented (Howe and Hinings, 1987; Howe, 1990; Logan and Hughes, 1995; Watson, 1995). We know that children entering late placements need to be helped with problems of continuity and loss (Fahlberg, 1994) and that people who have adopted older children frequently seek help with behavioural problems which include school difficulties, oppositional behaviour, verbal or physical abuse and moral or sexual risks (McGhee, 1995). We also know that the children's problems and the needs of parents vary over time, so that a sensitive response is required (Rushton *et al*, 1993).

In general, the findings of this study are consistent with those of Macaskill, who examined the post-placement needs of adopters of hard-to-place children during the 1980s (Macaskill, 1985). Information for her study was derived from interviews with adoptive parents and from file material at the London-based adoption agency, Parents for Children. She found that although the most acute problems were experienced by adopters in the early stages, the first and second years of placement were generally very active ones in which families 'enthusiastically channelled all their energy towards problem-solving' and considerable gains were made. During the third and subsequent years things moved at a slower but possibly more steady pace, and progress depended on the strength of the bond which had been formed between parent and child. At this stage she noticed that there was a lot of stability in some families, but there was also a risk of parental fatigue, if physical or emotional demands continued, and fresh difficulties could be introduced as the adopted children entered adolescence. Her final recommendation was for 'a long-term support service extending far beyond the formalisation of adoption'.

Since Macaskill's research there have been more detailed studies of children's development and social work help after adoption, However, these studies also show that the adoptive parents are active participants in the process, and that there is a need for careful negotiation 'in order to engage and hold them in effective help' (Rushton *et al*, 1993).

The single people in the study were proud of their own autonomy, and they had a strong desire to manage problems without recourse to professional agencies unless it was clearly required. They felt that they were not primarily consumers of services, but providers. It was in the immediate aftermath of the placement that the adopters were most likely to welcome professional help, and they chose whether to draw their main support at this time from the adoption agency worker or from the child's social worker. Most favourable comments were made about members of the adoption agencies, who had usually been involved in the approval of the adopter and continued to offer help, if necessary, on a 24-hour basis. However, in a few cases the children's social workers were found to be most helpful because of their knowledge of the background circumstances. In a few cases where a particularly good relationship had been formed, the children's workers were regarded as the main resource if things went wrong at a later stage.

Several months or years down the line, it was not adoption workers who provided the parents with professional support but routine services. For roughly one-third of parents the health services now included not only care from the general practitioner but regular visits to hospital so that the child could receive speech therapy and other treatments. The visits to schools to discuss the children's education or general welfare were extended to conversations with the educational psychologist, when the children had learning difficulties. Finally, there was occasional contact with Child and Family Guidance clinics or specialist therapeutic and counselling services when parents were worried by revelations of abuse and felt that such assistance was necessary. However, these visits happened somewhat rarely.

For six of the 15 sexually abused children, as we have already reported, counselling had been arranged or was already in progress. For another three of these children professional help was planned at a later date. Two had been given counselling or therapy while in the care system, while the remaining four were considered not to need treatment. No special help had been offered for physical or emotional abuse, regardless of severity.

Should more use have been made of the therapeutic services? Sometimes the right resource was not available, or access to it could not be arranged at the right time (art and play therapy are good examples). Social work help was more easily obtainable, but some of the adopters said that they would not readily accept help from social workers because of the risk of repeating unpleasant experiences for the child. Besides, people who had worked in the areas of health and social care were familiar with services such as Child and Family Guidance and they could have made contact directly. Sometimes they refrained because the child was strongly opposed to the idea, or because they were afraid of stigmatising the child.

Attitudes of the professional adopters

Because so many of the single adopters in the study were women and also professionals, one of the features of their post-adoption lifestyle was the way in which they combined both worlds. Even if they had worked in caring professions, they wanted to experience the spontaneous, informal care-giving which they felt to be central to their identity as women, and in fact this was one of the main reasons why they had sought to adopt. They relished the chance to do relatively ordinary tasks, such as helping with children's homework and planning trips to the seaside. The experience they gave the child was, in a broad sense, therapeutic, but they also "managed" the children's care, for example, by taking the initiative in seeking medical appointments, and they "paced" the introduction of counselling to match the children's apparent needs.

While exercising professional skills themselves, the adopters in the study were capable of holding the professional world at bay. Sometimes they seemed to do this to excess, but they had given the children in their care a way out from the official care system, and they were wary of any activity which might remind the child of past trauma or create the impression that "nothing changes". In some cases both parent and child seemed to be turning away from the depersonalising effects of corporate care.

By the time the adoption order was made, the adopters liked to regard themselves as self-sufficient. They were themselves taking action to meet their own needs, and since no contract for ongoing work had been entered into, there was a question about how much "post-adoption support" was required or justified.

One major consideration was the way in which it was offered. At times of family stress and change, or when the children's behaviour was exceptionally difficult, it might have been useful for more adopters to have access to a worker who knew the family, who was sympathetic to both parent and child, and who could be relied on to offer help and advice without undermining the placement. Professional support was also needed if the adopters had difficulty in managing contact with the birth family (see Chapter 13). In most other situations the adopters coped very well from their own resources, with the help of long-standing family members and friends.

Summary

- The single adopters did not always see themselves as entitled to official support. They felt privileged in being allowed to adopt, and they believed that they ought to cope with most problems themselves. They were also reluctant to involve professional agencies if there was a risk of making children feel different from others, or repeating experiences which the children had had in the care system.
- Most support came informally, from family and friends. This network provided both emotional and practical benefits for the adoptive parents and their children. Membership of the same network enabled the children to give as well as receive benefits.
- "Self-support groups" were valued by the few parents who used them. A group specifically arranged for adoptive parents was found to be more helpful than one for single parents, except where the latter was organised by a church to which the parent belonged. Clubs and organisations for children, together with holiday playschemes, were much in demand.
- The workers from the adoption agencies were a valuable source of advice in the early stages. The children's own social workers were most helpful if they knew a great deal about the children's

backgrounds. Prolonged contact with them was unusual, but in a few cases where a really good relationship had been established they maintained contact after the adoption.

- Extra help was most likely to be required at times of family reconstitution, or when there were extreme problems with children's behaviour, or when there was a disclosure of abuse. Professional support was also needed if the adoptive parents had difficulty in managing contact with the child's birth family. In most other situations the single adopters coped very well from their own resources.

12 Changes in the family over time

Throughout the course of the adoptions there were several ways in which the structure of adoptive families changed. Sometimes there was a death in the extended family. Sometimes a well-liked relative moved away, or an older child in the adoptive family left home, and the adopted child could experience this as a loss. On the other hand the extended family was increased by marriages, by partnerships and by births. In this way the adopted children experienced the family as "growing" around them. It was a very different experience from institutional care, with its mobile and yet chronologically fairly static population of children who came and went and were replaced by others of a similar age.

There were two forms of structural change which could be particularly unsettling because they affected the parent–child relationship directly. The first was when the parent adopted another child or a sibling group. The second was when the parent took a partner. (This did not happen very often, but when it did happen it was obviously extremely important.) Both of these events have parallels in natural families, and they also occur in two-parent adoptive households. There were, however, specific aspects of regroupings involving partners or siblings that appeared to be linked to the circumstances of the single adopters, and it is useful to explore their impact.

New siblings

Out of the 30 adopters in the study, there were 12 who had adopted more than once and another seven who expressed a wish to adopt again when their present child was older. Some of those who had already adopted more than once also said that they would like to adopt again for a third or fourth time. There was therefore a strong wish to have more than one child and in some cases more than two.

The adopters had fairly definite views about the optimum size for their family, but – as reported in Chapter 10 – economic factors could play a part in the decision. For three parents, withdrawal from work became financially feasible when a decision was made to adopt for the third time. Because of the needs of children in the care system, single adopters who wanted larger families may also have been encouraged to consider sibling groups. Of the 12 parents who had successfully applied to adopt more than once, eight had had one more child placed with them, but four parents had received two extra children or more. In two of these cases there was a placement involving sibling pairs.

Given the popularity of second placements, what was it that deterred some people from proceeding further? Of the 11 parents who had had one child placed with them and who said they would probably not adopt again, three had other children (usually older children of their own) and felt that the adopted child completed their family to their satisfaction. Another three said that it would be against the interests of the present child to adopt again because the child was exceptionally needy. For example, one parent stated:

> *I think Gary would have to become a great deal more mature, independent . . . He very easily starts to become attention-seeking, and he can become quite unkind [to other children] if he feels that he isn't getting the right attention.*

One woman who wanted to adopt again had applied and been rejected, ostensibly because her housing was unsuitable. The remaining four people had all found the adoption to be fairly demanding of their resources. Their available energy was being used up and they had decided that they could not cope with another child. It is interesting to note that in spite of much hard work and success, their enjoyment of the child was noticeably lower than that of the people who wanted to adopt again, and they had more reservations about the actions already taken. They also had high standards and were self-critical. One of these women said:

> *I should have looked deeper into the question of access to male company for a boy child.*

Another said:

> *Knowing what I know now, I wouldn't do it again, for a second child. But if it was for the first time, yes . . . I think you can survive and do OK.*

These people who had experienced the adoptive path as somewhat stony were predominantly white, professional women who had adopted older children. They had enormous personal qualities and skills, but they lacked specific child-care experience. (Two of them had worked in high positions in the health service.) They had struggled hard with the problems involved in parenting an older child from the care system, and although they felt that in large measure they had succeeded, the adoption had been more problematic than they had anticipated and they had no wish to repeat the experience.

Surprisingly, there were hardly any parents who suggested that they would not adopt again because the one-to-one relationship between themselves and their child was too fragile or important to be put at risk. The people who came nearest to it were three who said that adoption would be against the interests of the present child who was very demanding of their attention. Most parents regarded the presence of another child as an unmitigated benefit, as long as they had the personal resources to cope with the extra work involved.

This casts a new light on the notion of "one-to-one relationship" which was often used on official forms as a justification for single-person adoption. The adopters valued the relationship with their child but they did not regard it as being in any way exclusive, and it was certainly not compromised by the arrival of another child, although most people felt that it would be compromised by the arrival of a partner.

The experience of introducing new children to the family
Parents were generally well-prepared for a second adoption, and with careful introductions the new children slid easily into the households. The average time between one placement and the next was about four years. Either by accident or by design, therefore, the timing of the second placement fulfilled the dictum that in order to minimise the risk of placement breakdown, the placed child should be younger than any new step-sibling by at least three years (Wedge and Mantle, 1991).

The main complaint of second-time adopters was that the amount of work had increased, and for a brief period it could be quite excessive. They reported feelings of tiredness or difficulty in adjusting to the new routine, even when sufficient help was available. Once again, many of their experiences can be linked to those of natural parents who have just given birth to a second or third child. However, there were differences, which stemmed from the age of the children as well as the extent of their difficulties. An age gap of three to four years between adopted siblings seems natural enough, but when the first child is aged nine and the second is aged five, the decision is more complicated and demands a greater amount of family discussion than when the first child is aged three or four.

The fact that existing children responded remarkably well to the new child's arrival probably reflects the extent to which they had been involved in the selection process. Adolescent and pre-adolescent children were regularly given a "voice" when it came to choosing a second child, and in at least one case the child was given the right to veto the proposal. The adoptive parent said:

> In some ways it sounds as though I was placing a lot of emphasis on Gina not liking her [the proposed second child]. But it was important, because you have to make them gel.

It was not unusual to find a strong alliance between the parent and the first child at the time when a second placement was undertaken. Sometimes, however, the bond between the parent and the first child developed much more strongly *after* the second placement. There appear to be a number of reasons for this. Firstly, where the child had been directly involved in the preliminary discussions and had helped to choose a second child, the first child had become a partner in the parent's decision. This meant that the child had made an emotional investment in the placement, in much the same way as the parent had done, and was committed to working in partnership to make the new child feel at home. Secondly, the arrival of a child who was wanted and welcomed helped to cement the pre-existing relationship. Thirdly, the parents who adopted again after an interval of two years or more were suddenly made aware of the contrast between the children. This applied particularly to people who adopted older children with disturbed backgrounds. When they found that they were retracing familiar paths, in terms of stabilising difficult behaviour, this made them realise how much progress had been made in the *first* adoption.

As a result, their feelings of liking and sympathy for the first child increased. One single adopter said:

When Sarah was placed I really started to appreciate Louise, because of this other child and what a horror she was!

Although this attitude was helpful in preserving the original relationship as well as defusing any feelings of jealousy on the part of the first child, care had to be taken in case it resulted in a situation where there was difficulty in integrating the second boy or girl. (The notion of "triangulation" which is common in family therapy is useful as a way of understanding this pattern.) One parent admitted to having deep but temporary feelings of hostility towards her second adopted child, along with a strengthening of the bond between herself and the one who had been placed first.

There was a point when – well, I nearly sent Caroline back. I never felt that way with Mark.

Sibling groups

The children placed for adoption had often formed part of a group of siblings, who were the subject of parallel court applications. There is mounting evidence that joint placement of siblings can be beneficial to the children concerned (Rushton, *et al*, 1989). For single adopters, however, it was particularly hard work to establish relationships when the second placement involved siblings not related to the first child. Naturally enough, the new children formed a unit and they clung together for support (they had usually been placed together for that very reason). This meant that the first child tended to ally himself or herself even more clearly with the adoptive parent.

One parent who felt that she had made enormous progress with her first child, Marilyn, said that she found herself 'back to square one' with the sibling placement. Shortly after they entered the household, the new children began to "act out" in a very disturbed way and the situation called for physical restraint.

It was a bit like having Marilyn all over again, except I'd got three of them running round screaming . . . Flora [the older one of the sibling pair] was screaming because she thought I was hurting

> *Bess [her little sister] and Marilyn was screaming because she thought Bess was hurting me.*

As the adoptions progressed, these tensions became less. The adopted siblings tended to coalesce as a group and the first child would sometimes take the part of the others in discussions or arguments with the adoptive parent. The danger then was that the stronger of the children would draw the others into an alliance against the parent. (Two people whose children were on the verge of adolescence reported these fears.) However, the advantages of a strong alliance in the group of adopted children clearly outweighed the disadvantages, and the adoptive parents – even when they felt slightly threatened – had no wish to undermine it.

The adopters often worried that the older children would show signs of disturbance when there was a second placement, because the new children's arrival was likely to remind them of unpleasant experiences such as physical or sexual abuse. On the whole these worries were unjustified. The children who had been placed first were of course upset by revelations of abuse which resembled what they had suffered, but they were usually sympathetic when they recognised in another child the trauma of experiences similar to their own.

Partner relationships

None of the female adopters in the study were cohabiting but a few had a male friend in a permanently supportive role. These relationships appeared to be extremely stable. The male friend was friendly and helpful to both the child and the mother, and was recognised as having a special relationship which did not involve residence in the household. It was an arrangement which preserved the autonomy of both partners. It also preserved the consistency of experience which was necessary for some of the more insecure children, by leaving decision-making firmly in the hands of the adoptive mother.

Most women who were well established as adoptive parents said that marriage or cohabitation was unlikely, but that if they did want to enter a permanent partnership they would do so with great caution.

> *If I did meet somebody I would go into it very carefully, very gently, and we'd work something out. I can't see myself getting*

into any relationship with anybody who didn't take to Erica, so I don't think that would be a big problem.

One woman who had adopted two pre-adolescent daughters, one of whom had been sexually abused, said:
If somebody came along, that would be lovely. But they will not be a partner. They will be a friend.

The experience of new partnerships

There were only three parents in the study who entered a new and permanent partnership after the child was placed with them, in such a way that another adult was added to the household. Two of them were women who decided that they wanted to marry. The third was a man who had previously been divorced, and who was joined by a much younger woman. The only really successful match was the last one.

Several points of relevance to single-person adoption emerge from the adopters' accounts of these situations. Firstly, the women who took new partners had felt a certain amount of anxiety about bringing up an adopted child single-handed, and the feeling of inadequacy had been increased by experiences of rejection at the hands of local authorities. These experiences had convinced both these women that adoption is a privilege which should normally be reserved for married couples. Secondly, one of the main factors which destabilised the less successful partnerships was not the presence of the adopted child or children but complications involving natural and step-children. Thirdly, because of traditional expectations about the balance of power, the arrival of a father figure was experienced as somewhat threatening. Fourthly, both the female single parents who took partners were fairly isolated in terms of support, and although they coped positively with the problems of family reconstitution, there was a total absence of professional intervention at that time.

Since the outcome of the male adopter's partnership was encouraging, it seems relevant to ask what had contributed to it. In addition to the more obvious implications of gender role, the success of the arrangement appears to be due to the interaction of a number of factors. Firstly, the adoptive father was both committed and determined. Secondly, the change happened at a time when the parent–child relationship was well established and stable. Thirdly, there was a certain amount of official help available on a non-intrusive, non-interventionist basis. In addition to the support of the child's social worker, who had formed an unusually good relationship with the boy in care, this family had a lot of backing from the adoption agency which had completed the approval process. It was officially recognised that the father had a strong commitment to his adopted son, as well as to his partner, and he responded by restating that commitment without qualification.

The fourth factor to be taken into consideration is the family's lifestyle. The atmosphere within the family described above was warm and expressive, relaxed and easy going, with clear boundaries but without any rigid apportioning of tasks to men and women. The young woman's personality was such that she fitted easily into this household, not attempting to "smother" the adolescent boy or to repeat previous unhappy experiences, but offering him adult companionship (while retaining her position as his father's partner) and occasionally mediating between him and his father. Fifthly, all pre-existing relationships – including those between the adoptee and his father's ex-wife and her family – were respected and allowed to continue openly. There was a high level of activity and interaction not only between the members of the household but between the family and the working-class community of which they were a part.

In conclusion, it is clear that like other families, single adoptive households can be joined by new children or new partners and can be enriched by them. The problems uncovered here in connection with family reconstitution are not insuperable, nor are they specific to adoption. Nevertheless, the adoptive children and other children in the adopter's household were capable of being deeply affected by the arrival of new partners, and professional workers as well as friends and relatives may have a part to play in stabilising the family during this time of structural change.

Summary
* Through births and other events in the extended family, the adopted children experienced the new family as growing around them. Their

CHANGES IN THE FAMILY OVER TIME

interviews show that they enjoyed this experience.

- The main form of structural family change in the nuclear family was when the single parent adopted another child or a sibling group. The existing child was often involved in the selection process.

- Two sibling pairs were adopted by parents in the study, and in each case there was one other placed child. For a single adopter, this situation was particularly hard work to manage. However, the children appeared to benefit from joint placement.

- None of the female adopters in the study were cohabiting, although a few had a male friend in a permanently supportive role. These relationships appeared to be extremely stable.

- Only three new adult partnerships of any importance had been formed since the adoptions. Although common enough in the general population and probably less upsetting than divorce or separation (Wallerstein and Kelly, 1980), the planned entry of another adult to the single-person household was potentially unsettling for the children, and it needed careful management.

13 Contact with the child's birth family

Adoption policy has undergone a number of changes in recent years. One of these is the increasing recognition that "openness" is a viable proposition, especially when older children are placed for adoption, and that some form of contact with the birth family and previous carers can be beneficial.

The arguments for this belief are psychological, sociological, historical, legislative and moral. The key argument is probably a psychological one – namely that children are capable of forming multiple relationships, and that openness in adoption will help the child to develop a positive sense of personal and social identity. A subsidiary justification is that contact with the child may also be therapeutic for the birth parent, who sometimes needs help with the grieving process, while on-going contact prevents the build-up of unhelpful fantasies on both sides (Mullender, 1991; Adcock et al, 1993).

Other perspectives are helpful but less widely recognised. A more sociological approach to the issue of contact focuses on methods of dispute resolution, and encourages the belief that since children in divorce cases are helped by co-operation between the parties, adopted children may also be helped by the negotiation of non-adversarial relationships. It is also useful to approach the issue from a historical point of view – to see the effects of changes in our social situation since the 1920s, leading to a lessening of the need for secrecy to protect children from the stigma of illegitimacy or to protect parents from the shame of infertility. From the perspective of legal and moral rights, too, current practice derives authority from the principles underlying the Children Act 1989, with its emphasis on partnership and the continuation of parental responsibility for children in substitute care. A powerful influence on social work practice in this area has been the extension of arrangements for people to obtain information about their birth records, and the increase in provision for contact after the age of 18.

In spite of the wealth of legal and theoretical material which now seems to support contact with the birth family, there is still very little detailed empirical data on birth family contact in adoption, with the exception of the New Zealand studies carried out by Rockel and Ryburn (1988), the early work by Fratter (1989, 1991) and the more recent work by June Thoburn. The present study affords some opportunity to examine these issues, within the limits of the research design, since many of the single parents had adopted older children. Some of their experiences are probably unique to single parents, but others may be common to all cases where there is a transfer of parental rights, whether there is one parent or two.

The nature and extent of birth family contact

Sixteen children in the study (one-third of the sample) had face-to-face contact with one or more members of the birth family. When the placement was instigated, plans had been made for these children to retain contact with certain family members where this seemed to be in their interests. In practice the decision appeared to hinge upon whether there was a pre-existing relationship between the child and a birth relative which, in the opinion of the professionals, should not be broken.

Table 14
Face-to-face contact with members of the birth family

Relative in the birth family	No. of children who see this relative at least weekly N = 48	No. of children who see this relative less than weekly N = 48	Total no. of children who see this relative N = 48
Mother	–	7	7 (15%)
Father	–	3	3 (6%)
Grandparent	–	5	5 (10%)
Sibling	1	12	13 (27%)
Uncle or aunt	1	1	2
Great grandmother	–	2	2
Cousin	1	–	1

It is interesting to compare the information in Table 14, which charts the children's links with their birth families, with the corresponding information about children in their adoptive families (Table 13). As might be expected, the contacts with birth family members were much less frequent than those which took place with members of the adoptive family – less than weekly or monthly and usually no more than once or twice a year. The choice of contacts was also different. The birth relative whom the adopted child was most likely to see after the placement was not a parent or a grandparent but a sibling. Twenty-seven per cent of the children in the sample were in touch with one or more of their birth siblings. Eight children (one in six) were in touch with one or both of their birth parents, and only five children had the chance to see a grandparent from the birth family.

Face-to-face contact was not the only form of interaction between the adoptive family and the birth family, of course, since in some cases the professional agencies had set up a "postbox" system for the exchange of letters and photographs. Most of the adoptive parents said that they had met the birth parent on at least one occasion, whether or not contact was continued.

The introductory meeting between the adoptive parent and the birth parent

The prospective adopters were almost always keen to meet the birth parent (usually the mother) of the child they were planning to adopt, even though in two-thirds of cases there was no expectation of further contact before the child was 18. According to their own accounts, they were motivated by curiosity as well as sympathy, but they wanted to reassure the birth mother that the child would be well looked after and they also wanted to obtain her goodwill. They realised that the child might want to resume contact with her in adulthood, and they were prepared for this to happen.

Many of the single adopters felt genuinely sympathetic to the birth mother. The social worker had acquainted them with some of her problems, and as single women they had often shared them. They understood the financial and emotional pressures she had been subjected to, and they also understood some of her experiences at the hands of men. They sometimes found the meeting difficult. Nevertheless they contrived to make it a valuable and healing experience for all concerned.

Face-to-face contact with the birth parents

There were eight children who saw at least one of their birth parents on a regular basis. Of these, two children aged four and five had contact both with their birth mother and with their birth father. Five children between the ages of seven and 15 had contact with their birth mother only, and one girl who was aged 17 was in touch with her birth father.

In all of these cases the face-to-face contact was infrequent, although there was usually an exchange of letters and telephone calls in between the visits. The 17-year-old girl had seen her father once in the last year. The children who had access to their birth mother saw her twice a year, and the other two children had contact with their birth parents three or four times a year.

In order to understand the impact of contact in these adoptions, it is necessary to look more closely at the situations represented here.

Contact with both the birth parents

The two small children who were regularly in touch with both their birth parents were usually taken to see them by their adoptive mother, although at other times they were visited by them and by other relatives. Both the children had Down's Syndrome. They also had the same adoptive mother, although they came from different birth families. One of the factors pre-disposing this family to "open adoption" must have been her willingness to incorporate birth parents in the lives of her children. She said in her interview:

> I love the parents very much. They're very good friends of mine. I mean, they gave me their most precious possession, didn't they?

She also said:

> They adore their children. They just don't feel that they can bring them up.

The birth parents in these two cases were fully supportive of the adoption and had chosen it in preference to other options. They wanted their

125

disabled children to have the security of adoption, which freed them to care for other children in the family. At the same time, they welcomed the opportunity to have occasional contact with their adopted children, an experience which may have alleviated any lingering feelings of guilt or anxieties about the children's welfare, and they also appreciated the fact that they were being allowed to participate in the children's upbringing while the main work of physical and emotional caring was being done by someone else. The two sets of birth parents, who were unrelated, also gained strength and companionship from being introduced to one another. (They saw the other disabled siblings during visits to the household, and occasional meetings between the families were arranged.) The adoptive mother, for her part, felt encouraged by their respect and admiration. She also found the input of the parents to be of real practical help, which in one case was being extended to include respite care.

Visits to these children seem to have been made easier by the children's ready acceptance of the arrangements and the absence of any necessity for complicated explanations. The adoptive mother described the children's awareness of the roles and relationships as follows:

> Colin [the five-year-old Down's Syndrome boy] just knows that his birth mother is someone very, very special. We call her 'Mummy Pat' and in the same way we call Michael's mother 'Mummy Jane'. And of course both of them have Daddies, but we don't have a Daddy, so that doesn't confuse them.

The single adoptive mother – like the female social worker who had preceded her – tended to find it easier to form a good relationship with the birth mother rather than with the birth father. In other cases where there was a dominant and critical male in the child's original household (regardless of whether the criticism was directed at the child or the birth mother or the adoptive parent), contact was discontinued.

Contact with the birth father

There was only one child in the study who was in touch with her birth father but not her birth mother, and the situation was complicated by the fact that visits were resumed after a long interval. Since this girl was 17 years old, some of her difficulties probably mirrored those of children who make contact with their birth parents in adulthood, but at the time when contact was renewed she was still living with her adoptive mother.

At the time of our interviews, face-to-face contact had only recently been initiated. The girl wanted to see her father, but the adoptive mother was less than keen on the meeting. As far as she was concerned, the timing and the orientation were both wrong.

> *She's met her father and he's told her certain things, which she's now decided she needs counselling for. So she's going to see somebody. But if there's some way that Sharon can get attention, Sharon will do it.*

In this case the adoptive mother was wary of introducing changes which might destabilise the situation. As far as she was concerned, she had worked hard to give a sense of permanence and consistency to a very disturbed girl, and she resented what she felt to be the ill-effects of "dragging up the past". This woman had herself been abused as a child, and her methods of survival were different from those which her daughter was now attempting to use. She equated extensive "counselling" with self-indulgence.

In terms of the categorisation in Chapter 7, this adoptive mother was one of the "old hands". She would probably have preferred a traditional type of adoption with complete cut-off from the birth family.

Other adopters expressed worries about face-to-face contact with birth fathers for different reasons, and in some cases there would have been danger to both mother and child because of the risk of physical violence. In view of these difficulties, we feel justified in identifying this situation as one which may be particularly problematic for single women who adopt.

Contact with the birth mother

Natalie, who was aged ten, had enjoyed uninterrupted contact with her birth mother and her half-sister (albeit infrequently) since her birth, and she found no problems in having the relationship recognised. The adults and children were able to meet and enjoy each other's company for two weeks in the summer holidays every year. These occasions were valued and the arrangements worked.

The birth mother in this case was actually a relative of the adoptive mother. This close association between the families undoubtedly helped, but the adoptive mother said that although Natalie recognised the biological relationship between herself and the birth mother, the main bond was definitely between her and the child. In illustration, she said that when they were both present in the room Natalie always turned to her in preference to the other woman when she needed advice or comfort or corroboration:

> *... mainly because there isn't that tension between us, and perhaps because I have got more parenting skills.*

She also felt that Natalie respected the relationship between her biological mother and her half-sister, and expected her half-sister to turn to her own mother in the same way that she did. Generally speaking these unwritten rules were observed.

The girl herself made it clear that she was happy in the company of all these people, whom she regarded as close family members. She said in her interview that her adoptive mother was her 'Mum' and that her birth mother was 'more like an aunty, sort of thing'. In clarification of this remark she added, 'I do know she's my real Mum; but I see her as an aunty'. Her one regret was that she did not see her birth mother and half-sister more often.

> *We talk to them on the phone nearly every Sunday but it's not the same as seeing them.*

The other four children who had contact with their birth mother at the time of our interviews had not yet been formally adopted. This meant that the situation was still fluid, although plans had been made, and there was more anxiety about contact. In the case of one sibling placement of a 15-year-old girl and her 14-year-old sister, the single carer was seeking to end or severely curtail face-to-face contact on the grounds that the girls themselves did not want to see their birth mother and found the visits distressing.

> *We would go along for contact. Sometimes she would turn up,*

> *sometimes she wouldn't. It was terribly upsetting, and we all thought it would be best if we just had contact by letter while they're growing up.*

A guardian *ad litem* had been appointed in this case and it seemed likely that contact would be terminated.

The remaining children – a girl aged seven and a boy aged ten – both had access to their birth mothers regularly and they were both in recent placements which were carefully supervised. Both had feelings of divided loyalty, but the prospective adoptive parents were sensitive to the children's feelings about their birth family, and aware of their sense of helplessness. The adopter of the ten-year-old boy said:

> *He'll never instigate things. But out of the blue, when he's in the middle of the swimming pool or something, he'll say, 'Oh, I must send my Mum a Christmas card.' It's obviously been on his mind for weeks, and he suddenly blurts it out.*

Although they understood the need for continued contact with the birth mother, these parents also had anxieties and some reservations. Being highly committed as future parents, they wished to preserve face-to-face contact with the birth mother if it was in any way a resource for the children whom they were undertaking to adopt. Their main complaint was that the resource which they saw offered by the birth parent was so limited.

Face-to-face contact with birth siblings and other relatives

In 13 out of the 16 cases where the adoptee had contact with one or more members of the birth family, there was interaction with at least one birth sibling. Usually the child saw more than one, for example, two brothers, or a brother and a sister. There was some contact with grandparents in addition, but in most of the cases in the study, children and young people carried the main brunt of the liaison between the different families. The reverberations of this notion are quite considerable.

Because of the extent to which birth family members were in touch with each other, official meetings to discuss access arrangements could be incredibly complicated. Siblings were almost always on the agenda and because the siblings were children their interests had to be balanced. One adoptive parent who was present at such a discussion said that she managed to be 'clear-headed' about the fact that no access to the birth parents should be allowed in the case of her adopted daughter, but she was less certain about a request for access to the grandparents because another child was involved. (The eldest daughter lived with the grandparents.) Her comments were:

> I tried to stay clear-headed throughout the meeting. I thought:
> 'The grandparents aren't under consideration here.' But I was
> having to sort it out as I went.

There seemed to be two main situations in which face-to-face contact with siblings and other relatives took place. Firstly, there were six cases where the adopted child saw one or more relatives – usually siblings or half-siblings but sometimes grandparents – in addition to the birth parent. In these cases the contact with other relatives was secondary to the contact with the natural parent, and it sometimes had a lower priority. In eight other cases contact with a sibling or grandparent was arranged in its own right. Sometimes these birth relatives may have had a role in representing the family, although it is safer to assume that they were negotiating their own relationships with the adopted child.

Meetings with siblings and grandparents as an adjunct to parental contact

Where the adoption was very "open", it was not unusual to find that family access meetings were attended by a number of relatives. In the case of the two children with Down's Syndrome described above, the birth parents were accompanied on visits by the adopted children's natural brothers and sisters, and there was also occasional unplanned contact with grandparents, aunts and uncles. The ten-year-old Natalie, as already mentioned, saw her half-sister along with her birth mother.

One other adopter who had very "open" meetings with the birth family gave this account of the twice-yearly contact visits which were arranged at a local access centre.

> *There are usually about 12 people there. Family, friends,*

neighbours . . . You never know what to expect, because they bring all sorts of people along to see him [the adopted child]. It's a big family day out for them, bless them.

This meeting happened no more than twice a year, but it was frequent enough for the adopter who found it boring and rather stressful. Several members of the birth family, including the mother, had learning difficulties which made conversation difficult, and there seems to have been a clash of cultural values as well.

It's quite fraught – not through aggression, but because there's no real conversation. I talk to her [the birth mother] and she listens. Jerry goes off and plays with his brother. Me and the social worker have to keep it going for two or three hours.

When commenting on the relationships in the above case, the adopter described the child's feelings as follows:

His Mum is his Mum. He's still got something for her.

She admitted, on the other hand, that the child preferred to spend the access visit playing with his brother, and that he also liked to spend time with his older sister. This same pattern is reported by other adopters. For example, a woman with two teenage daughters said of one of them:

She goes back to see Andy and Maureen [her brother and sister], not to see her Mum.

In some but not all of these cases it does seem as though the sibling contact was of more value to the child than the adult contact. Allowance must be made for the feelings of the adoptive parents, who may have preferred this interpretation of events because they felt more threatened by the presence of the birth parents. However, there is also support for the same viewpoint in the children's interviews. Ten-year-old Jerry, for example, said that he would like to see his brothers more often and that he was especially pleased to discover that his sister was expecting a baby. (He looked forward to becoming an uncle.) It was frustrating for him to be limited to twice-yearly visits to his siblings. He knew that his birth family was not allowed to come to his present address, but he did not really understand why.

Contact with other relatives in their own right

There were eight cases of face-to-face contact which did not include visits to or by the birth parents. Five involved access to siblings only, and in one other case the child had access only to a grandparent. In the remaining two cases, one of which was a family situation involving adoption by the child's paternal aunt, both siblings and grandparents were included in access arrangements.

Apart from the single adopters' willingness to participate, there seem to have been a number of reasons why these particular family members were encouraged to stay in touch or resume contact with the adopted child, when contact with the birth parents had been discontinued.

Firstly, there were some relatives – particularly older siblings and grandparents – who had actually fulfilled a parental role in relation to the child. The links with these relatives had usually emerged by a kind of evolutionary process during the children's care history, and by the time of the adoption placement some patterns of access were well-established. Where contact with the children's birth parents had been terminated or allowed to wither in the course of the children's pre-placement experiences, the links with siblings or grandparents in these situations had often been kept alive.

Secondly, there were child protection issues. Some children were deemed to have been abused or badly neglected by their birth parents, and official action had been taken to separate them. In a few of these cases it was felt that face-to-face contact with the birth parent or parents was too dangerous to be allowed; however, sibling contact was seen as beneficial, if only because the siblings had shared some of the same parenting experiences.

Thirdly, the children and their siblings had often been accommodated together in foster care or residential homes and they had clung together for support. As a result, they had a very close bond and a continuing need to see each other, if only to verify that the other brothers and sisters were not being harmed.

Fourthly, a purely practical consideration appeared to be the feasibility of arranging contact with siblings without allowing this contact to "spread" and encompass other members of the birth family. If the child's siblings had been adopted or fostered, it was possible to arrange access through official channels without the risk of other family members becoming involved.

There were, additionally, a few cases in which family contact had been lost, to the detriment of the child's interests, and sibling contact was seen as a way of recovering it. For example, in one case of sexual abuse to a young girl, the child had not only been separated from her father who was responsible for the incidents but from her mother and siblings as well. Both the social worker and the adoptive mother were keen to extend the girl's contact with the birth family, and reunion with one of the child's brothers was seen as a necessary and feasible first step.

For all these reasons, contact with siblings and sometimes grandparents was encouraged. In most cases it was extremely beneficial and the adopters supported it. There were only a few situations which posed problems for the adopters. The first was where the siblings had not only been sexually abused by others but were suspected of having abused each other. (In one case of this sort, the abuse was alleged to have taken place in residential care, but did not come to light until after the contact plans had been drawn up.) The second was where siblings had privileged access to other family members, which tempted them to seek power by spreading gossip and also made them feel superior to the adopted child. The third was where different contact arrangements were seen to be needed for children who lived in the same adoptive family.

For some women living on their own with small children, the risk of physical violence from members of the birth family (if the address were to be disclosed) was an ever-present worry. However, even indirect contact could pose problems because of the perceived necessity to filter out harmful information. Whether or not the adopters had anxieties about face-to-face contact, the children who were interviewed usually valued this movement across the boundary between the adoptive family and the birth family and they wanted it to continue.

Summary

- Various theoretical perspectives now seem to support the continuation of contact with the birth family after a child is adopted – particularly where there is a pre-existing relationship which needs to be safeguarded.
- The single adopters had many anxieties about birth family contact. Some of these anxieties were focused on possible harm to the child or the undermining of the parent–child relationship. Others were more concerned with secondary spin-offs, such as the effect on other members of the household.
- One issue of importance to single women adopters was the protection which needed to be offered to themselves and their children, if an adult member of the birth family was known to be violent.
- The birth relative whom the adopted child was most likely to see after the placement was a sibling. Twenty-seven per cent of the children in the sample were in touch with one or more of their birth siblings. Only one in six saw their birth mother, and fewer saw the birth father.
- The arrangements for face-to-face contact were most successful when there was a total absence of conflict, for example, in the case of disabled children whose adoption had been actively sought by the birth parents. Face-to-face contact was least successful when the adoptive parent regarded the birth family with strong disapproval.
- Even indirect contact could be difficult for the adopters to sustain because of the perceived need to filter written information. However, the children were the main beneficiaries of both direct and indirect contact, and they generally wanted the arrangements to continue.

14 The experiences of the children

As reported in Chapter 4, 21 children over the age of six were interviewed. The questions asked during the interviews were not simply about adoption. The children were invited to talk about other things that were important to them, for example, friends and relatives, hobbies and interests. A picture was obtained of comparatively "normal" children, who liked to see their friends and to take part in activities outside the home. It is easy to overlook these significant features in the lives of adopted children, by concentrating too hard on the aspects of adoption which are particularly painful to discuss.

Views about the parent's single status
The interviews gave us a chance to ask children directly about what they felt to be the impact of their adoptive parent's single status. Most children felt that there was no particular disadvantage associated with having one parent, and they did not feel themselves to be significantly different from other children who had two. However, their responses varied with age and understanding.

5–9 age group
The children in the younger age group usually accepted the structure of their adoptive family as normal without making comparisons. A few children, however, counted it as an actual advantage to have one parent because it made life simpler and conflict-free. Nine-year-old Suzanne said that in her family it was peaceful and there were no headaches. The ability to have decisions made without having to reconcile the wishes of two different adults was another advantage, because it gave a lot of flexibility as well as consistency to the family's planning. Six-year-old Jacqueline, who said that she had been 'to Tunisia and to netball', felt that she was able to do a lot of interesting things, because having a single mother increased the opportunity for both of them to engage in outside

activities. This feeling was by no means uncommon.

Both boys and girls in the five to nine age group seemed to be happy with their general situation and lifestyle – apart from some good-humoured grumbles about household rules – and consequently they had no specific complaint about living in a single-parent household. Only a very few children, such as eight-year-old William, had tried hard to identify a father figure among their mother's friends or associates.

The young children who openly sought a father-figure had not experienced one in the birth family, and it is interesting to note that they were apparently not motivated solely by their own needs but by concern for what they imagined to be the needs of their adoptive parents. Samuel, a nine-year-old boy with learning difficulties, had become actively involved in checking out his mother's male friends with a view to finding her a suitable partner. He decided that he liked one particular man whom they had met on a camping holiday. 'If you were thinking of getting married,' he said tactfully to his adoptive mother, 'I think he would do.'

10–15 age group

Children aged 10 to 15 had more experience of other children's families, and they were capable of making a realistic assessment of what life might be like in a different family structure. Twelve-year-old Alexander, who lived in a large black family, felt that a father would simply be 'an extra person'. (He had an adequate male role model in his older brother.) Thirteen-year-old Maria complained that in a single-parent household there was 'less money in the family'. However, ten-year-old Natalie said that her best friend who lived in a two-parent family appeared to be in a similar position to herself, since this friend's father spent most of his time at work and the only person she saw regularly when she visited the house was her friend's mother. Other children had noticed that mothers were the people most likely to take children to hospital, to attend parents' evenings and to take part in school activities.

The children in the 10–15 age group had often thought deeply about their parent's marital status and they were capable of giving very considered responses. Ten-year-old Gail pointed out that it mattered who the single parent *was*. She did not object to single parenthood as such, but she was not willing to exchange her much-loved adoptive mother for another of unknown origin. The gender of the single parent was also important. One boy who had been placed for adoption a year ago, at the age of nine, had said during the selection process that he preferred to have 'a mother only' rather than 'a father only'. He appreciated the fact that these wishes had been respected.

Older children, and especially girls, sometimes felt that gender matching was an aid to the achievement of relaxed, intimate relationships. One adolescent girl who had been adopted by a single woman commented on the single-parent issues as follows:

> *It depends which parent it is. If it's two girls [that is, a mother and an adopted daughter] then it's good because you can just go around the house without worrying about having to wear anything, because that's what we're like. It all depends. If you've got a father and you're a girl then you might feel a bit embarrassed as you're getting older, but it depends.*

There was some support for gender matching, too, from a 14-year-old boy who lived happily with a single mother but went out a great deal with the adoptive father of one of his friends. Referring mainly to sports activities, he said:

> *There are some things you can do best with a Dad.*

It is interesting to note that in all cases where the child appeared to be actively searching for a father figure, that child was a boy. However, many of the girls in the study enjoyed the company of brothers, uncles and grandfathers, in addition to having frequent contact with adult male family friends and other people outside the household. Male company was not unimportant to them.

The lack of a father figure seemed to be felt more strongly by boys or girls if the single adoptive mother herself believed that two parents would have been better than one. In these cases the woman regarded herself as "less eligible" to adopt, and more privileged in being selected. This feeling of deficit may have transmitted itself to the child.

The significance of abuse

In the research sample as a whole, 42 per cent of the children (19 out of

48) had a background of known abuse, either physical or sexual, and in six cases they had suffered both. One child had been subjected to serious emotional abuse in the form of parental rejection. Several others had a background of minor emotional abuse and chronic neglect.

Table 10 gives the breakdown of types of abuse according to gender. It will be seen that the incidence of sexual abuse in the backgrounds of the children is very high, and that girls were the main victims. All of these girls were adopted by single women. Their ages at placement ranged between six and 11.

Girls who had been sexually abused, such as Gail (10) and Lucy (13), felt particularly at home with a single mother and felt sheltered and healed by this experience. One such child, who had been sexually abused by her father over a long period, said of her adoptive parent:

She won't let him or anyone else do that to me again.

In other words, the adoptive mother was offering protection and restoring to normality what had been an abnormal situation.

Another young girl who had been sexually abused for several years in the birth family specifically asked for a single mother when adoption was being contemplated. At the time of our interviews she was aged 13. She had no trouble in answering questions about her mother's single status, but she said that she still found it difficult to talk to schoolfriends of the circumstances surrounding her adoption. In fact she preferred to be regarded by her peers as illegitimate (a status which did not carry any stigma as far as she was concerned), rather than to reveal the fact that she had been adopted as a result of sexual abuse.

People at school ask me why I don't have a Dad, and because I don't want them to know about everything I'll just say, 'because I was born like it'. I'll just say I didn't have a Dad in the very best beginning [sic].

This example reminds us that what was most feared by the children was not the feeling of being different from the others but the feeling of being stigmatised.

Triseliotis has written of the way in which adoption lacked public acceptability in the early years of this century because of 'the general hostility and moral outrage felt towards the single mother at the time' ((Triseliotis, 1970). The children in our study did not seem to feel any impact of moral outrage about single parenthood. However, there is more than one reason for children to feel blamed. There is ample evidence that parents who become involved in the child protection system feel humiliated and condemned, and that this feeling of blame can be transmitted to the children if they are made to feel responsible for provoking the abuse in the birth family, or for bringing about the break-up of the family and the punishment of the abuser by means of public disclosures (Cleaver and Freeman, 1995; Farmer and Owen, 1995).

Not all of the abused children in the study carried a burden of guilt of this magnitude, of course, and where it had previously existed, sensitive treatment had in many cases helped to alleviate it. Nevertheless, for some severely abused children the notion of being brought up by a single mother was not only harmless but inviting. The only stigma which they continued to carry after the adoption (in some cases secretly) was concerned with the abuse itself.

The sexually abused girl who was quoted above said 'I've told people I can really trust' (about the background to her adoption). Her account continues:

> *When I told my best friend what had happened she thought it was disgusting, and that it would upset me if she told anyone else. She's right. But it's nice to be adopted because you feel like you have a normal home.*

Missing people

One issue of recurring importance to the children was the issue of missing people. In the course of the interviews we explored the children's feelings about people they might have lost, and also about people they felt they lacked in their present family. Needless to say, the answers to these two questions were different.

Most children had never known their birth father, or had known him only briefly when they were too young to remember him. If he had been known, he had often been an abuser. Perhaps in consequence of this, there were few children who suffered badly from the loss of this person or felt him to be important. The person from the past who was most regularly missed by people adopted beyond babyhood was the birth *mother*. Young children were capable of recounting the stories they had been told about her, sometimes without pain, but children who had been placed for adoption when they were on the verge of adolescence were particularly conscious of the birth mother's absence and featured her sensitively in their drawings. Second to this, the older adopted children missed their birth siblings and occasionally grandparents. The sense of loss surrounding these previous family members – and sometimes previous carers from foster homes or residential establishments – was capable of remaining, even when there were other people in the adoptive family who were well-liked and who regularly performed these roles.

When we turn to the members of the adoptive family, the situation is different. As might be expected, the children had more painful feelings about people they had *lost* than about people they simply *lacked*, especially if the notion of the missing person was based on a stereotype rather than on knowledge of someone they had previously loved or admired. There were, however, a few children who felt that they would have benefited from the presence of other family members.

The most commonly reported deficit in the adoptive family was not the lack of a father-figure or mother-figure but the absence of siblings. This lack could of course be made up by further adoptions, and in many cases this had happened already or else it was clearly on the agenda. Adoptive parents were aware of their children's need for companionship, where it existed, and they were also aware that status needs were sometimes involved. One ten-year-old girl told us jokingly that 'it would be good to have lots of younger children around so as you can beat them up'! However, a few children who had initially felt burdened by the solitariness and intensity of the relationship with the single parent might have welcomed the feeling of entering a larger nuclear family.

Two children who had expressed a wish for brothers and sisters at the time of the adoption, and who felt that their wishes had been ignored, felt particularly strongly on this issue. Both of them had come from large birth families. One of them was a young boy, recently placed, who said:

I wish there was somebody else here . . . another child . . . a boy.

The other was a teenage girl who said that she had asked for 'a mother, a father, a brother, a sister, a baby and lots of pets'. She admitted that her demands had been unrealistic, but she felt that they might have been given more attention. Her response to the selection of a new family was:

> I asked for all those things and what did I get? One mother and one pet!

The children's understanding of adoption

In our interviews with children we explored their knowledge of the reasons why they had been adopted, and also their understanding of adoption in general. These discussions introduced many more difficulties than were revealed by a simple consideration of the parent's single status. Consequently we feel justified in saying that for most children the fact of having a single parent was potentially less problematic than the fact of being adopted, and that adoption itself was most problematic for children who had entered their new families after experiences of abuse, neglect, parental rejection or constant disruption.

5–9 age group

As might be expected, the extent to which young children had grasped the difficult concept of adoption depended on age, experience and cognitive ability (Brodzinsky *et al*, 1986, 1990). It also depended on interest. Young black children were particularly unconcerned about adoption when their adoptive parents had a very relaxed but open attitude towards it and did not see a need to discuss it at great length. For these children it was important to know that they were adopted and to have some personal explanation of why they had left their birth families (for example, because their birth mother was very young or had too many children, while the adoptive parent had no children), but fuller explanations could safely be made to wait until they had acquired a more reflective and analytic approach to the world.

The extent and importance of previous experiences, and the age at which the children entered the household, clearly made a difference. Older children, whether black or white, were more likely to be reminded of their change of status by contact with previous relatives, but whether or not this continuing liaison existed, they had fuller memories of the time before they were adopted.

Some children in the 5–9 age group were reluctant to discuss these issues and we did not press them to do so. Among the children who did not want to talk much about adoption there were some who did not seem particularly interested, but there were also others who appeared to have been healed or defended themselves by forgetting. One nine-year-old child said:

> *When I left home I was six, but living here has just taken my memory away.*

Because of the complexity of adoption, young children (and also those who were older but had learning difficulties) tended to focus on one aspect of the concept and treat it as the whole. For children who had suffered numerous changes of placement in the past, the central point of adoption was *permanence*. Since this had probably been emphasised by their key workers, it is interesting to note that it comes through in the children's statements. Permanence was sometimes conceived in spatial or geographical terms. In other words adoption made it possible for them to stay in one place, instead of being moved constantly from one home to another. For others, the main value of adoption lay in the *quality of care* which they received, and permanence implied that they would be cared for 'always' or 'all the time'. Children who had been moved after unsatisfactory experiences of fostering or residential care (and in two cases after adoption breakdown) were glad to have exchanged a climate of coldness and hostility for a warm and supportive environment.

"Before and after" views of adoption were often polarised in young children's explanations and this polarisation was linked to a notion of moral worth. Whether or not the child had suffered abuse or neglect in the past, the adoptive parent was seen as a "good" parent who cared about children and did not commit abuse. When asked if anyone should be prevented from adopting, the children brought forward a view of child care which would have found acceptance with most moral welfare agencies from Victorian times to the present day.

> *[Who should not be allowed to adopt?] People who hit their children, or don't feed them and don't look after them properly. You need to be nice and kind.*

If I was choosing an adoptive parent, I would choose my Mum. Apart from that, I would choose someone who didn't smack and shout – unless she shouted for fun.

I think single-parent people should be able to adopt, and I think nearly everybody should be able to adopt, apart from people who are a bit mean and hit their children.

10–15 age group

Many of the children in the 10–15 age group had experienced both disruption and rejection prior to placement, and they had developed their own individual coping mechanisms. At the time of our interviews some of them were negotiating or renegotiating their relationship with the single carer, but they were also still processing difficult issues from the past. One 13-year-old girl said that her adoptive mother was 'a saint' and she acknowledged pushing her 'to the limits' as she gradually came to terms with the loss of her birth mother. When her adoptive mother criticised the birth mother, she said, that was what upset her most.

Occasionally there was a child who appeared to be using metaphor to describe difficult experiences, such as the 14-year-old disabled boy who had been neglected and abused both in the birth family and in foster care. He regularly answered questions about adoption by talking about the pain of wasp stings, the danger of infection from unclean wounds, and the paradoxical behaviour of wounded animals – even budgerigars.

Guess what? Budgerigars can bite. Do you know why they bite? It's that if the bird is dying and the beak is still there, sometimes that beak makes the little nip – and then the nip makes the bird die.

The accounts of these older children, many of whom had been adopted late, show that they had often felt confused and distressed at the time of placement. With hindsight, they were particularly conscious of their own powerlessness in relation to adoption. It seemed to them that they had had no part to play in the plans which were being made about them, and all the decisions had been made by adults, particularly social workers.

One 11-year-old girl who had joined her adoptive family two years earlier, after a history of deprivation which included both physical and emotional neglect, had this to say of the placement decision:

> *I was staying with foster parents and I kept going home and back again. Then the social worker said I had to leave there and belong to a Mum.*

Another child, a ten-year-old boy, said:

> *The social worker said I had to get adopshioned [sic]. I was a bit scared at first, but it was all right.*

A 14-year-old boy remembered feeling totally confused at the time of his placement when he was five years old, but he was also capable of distinguishing this from his present thinking.

> *I felt confused. I didn't know what was happening, or why I was here. Mind you, I was young then. It depends what age you are. If you're like my age now, you know what's going on.*

If children remembered being asked whether they wanted to be adopted, they sometimes said that they had been asked for their opinions by the social worker, but slightly more said that their adoptive parent had been the one to question them on the subject. This tallies with other research findings which suggest that social workers are sometimes reluctant to seek children's views (Murch *et al*, 1991). In the study of adoption processes by Murch *et al*, practitioners were asked whether they regarded it as part of their role to ascertain children's wishes and feelings about their situation. Over two-thirds of the social workers (70 per cent) replied that in the specific case the child was too young to discuss these issues. Of the remainder, only 19 per cent said that they did see it as part of their role. Four per cent claimed that it was not their business and the rest were unsure.

The older children in this study accepted the lead role which had been taken by social services, but they appreciated it when their wishes had been consulted and taken into consideration at the time of the placement. One articulate 11-year-old who felt that he had known what he wanted said:

> *I just wanted someone mature and agreeable – someone who lived*

*in a quiet street with bumpy roads for my BMX bike – and I found
her!*

These views presented a positive but challenging framework within
which the parent set out to build a realistic relationship with the child.
The drawings and the brief personal histories which follow will give a
deeper understanding of the experiences of individual children.

Ben

Ben is aged 12. He is the adopted brother of Martin, who is also
adopted, and he has been a member of the household for 18 months.
He chose to represent his family and friends in stick-figure form, but
they are arranged in groups, and there is a sense of proportion in his
choice of sizes. He recognises, for example, that his older brother is
bigger and probably stronger than himself. (In his interview he
referred to occasional 'scraps' which his mother had to referee.)

Ben's drawing is unusual in that he included a social worker next to
his adoptive family in the top row. He had clearly found her
sympathetic. At the time of the adoption he had also seen another
person who was 'like half a social worker, but not a social worker'.
He was uncertain of this person's identity and of the exact reasons for
adoption.

He did not mind having a single parent. For Ben, the central point
about adoption was permanence. In early childhood he had been
moved around a great deal from one relative to another, and even his
experience of long-term fostering had not lasted long. Adoption had
been explained to him as being 'like when you're fostered, but you
stay with the people forever'. He reasoned that 'it would be good, to
save moving around and all that'. However, he worried about who
would want to adopt him and what this person might be like. He also
worried about where he would be living. Even when he had met his
new parent and liked her, it took him some time to accommodate to
the idea of living in a major city.

*It was fun in the countryside because you could get really close to
the animals, and if you were quiet enough you could get close to
the cows and stroke them, but here you could get from this wall to*

Ben's drawing

MUM

Ben

Martin

Social worker

Neighbours

Schoolfriends

Dad   Mum

Birth parents

that wall [indicating distance] from a bird and they would hear you and fly away.

One of the most interesting features of Ben's drawing is that it contains his birth parents. He added them in the bottom left-hand corner, saying that he could briefly remember them. His birth mother died when he was aged seven or eight, and his birth father lives 'somewhere up in the North'. He would like to know more about his father and his birth siblings.

Unfortunately Ben's natural father has disappeared and much of his family history has been lost, but soon after the adoption his new mother took him on a visit to the North, where he made contact with his paternal grandmother and planted a rose on his mother's grave. This event may have helped him to come to terms with his grief. At any rate, it is encouraging to find that both his birth parents are represented here along with his family and friends.

Alexander

Like Ben, Alexander is aged 12. He is a cheerful black boy whose birth parents were African-Caribbean. His adoptive mother is of Nigerian origin. She sometimes calls her son by a Nigerian name, which he likes.

Alexander has lived in the adoptive home for about eight years. He had previously been fostered with a white family, but he identified strongly with black people, and when it became apparent that rehabilitation with his birth family was out of the question, a black family was sought for him. He has just started secondary school and is making new friends. Some of them are white, some African-Caribbean or Asian, and a few of mixed parentage.

It was clear to us that Alexander was proud of his cultural heritage, and that he felt he belonged in this family. He talked fondly of the various family members as he drew. His adoptive grandmother, who lives in Nigeria, is quite an important person in his eyes. He visited her last year and thinks about her a lot. His adoptive mother, who is a widow, is drawn next to him in the centre of the picture, and his younger adopted brother is between him and Sophie the cat (another

Alexander's drawing

important family member). On the right are the two natural children of his adoptive mother – a young man of 23 and a young woman of 21. Alexander gets on very well with both of them, and is thrilled about the fact that he now has a baby niece, who is depicted above in her cot.

Alexander's picture reflects his strong sense of belonging. The clothes worn by the nuclear family members are so similar that they could almost be a uniform, although there is clear differentiation of the sexes and some interesting individual detail. His foster parents are included in a circle above, as are some of his friends. He said that he liked the foster parents and used to telephone them regularly.

Alexander has not seen either of his birth parents for a very long time, and there are no plans for contact. His view of adoption is that it happens because somebody (usually a woman) wants a child. Adoptive parents want to look after children and 'keep them like they were real parents'. He thought that was probably the main reason why he had come to join his adoptive mother.

He sometimes thinks or dreams about his 'other family' and wonders what they might look like, but they did not have time for him, and so he felt that they must have agreed willingly to the adoption. They would have seen that it was best for him. He now has what he calls 'a proper family'. What would it be like to have a Mum and a Dad? 'It might be the same', he said. 'Just with one extra person.'

William

William is another boy of African-Caribbean parentage, and he is aged eight. He has been adopted almost from birth. He did not want to draw his family as he said he was not good at drawing people. Instead, he wrote down their names and their ages, and underneath the list of family members he put the names of his three best friends.

William wrote his own name first, and then the name of his adoptive mother, Veronica. Iris is his adoptive grandmother. The two-year-old Thomas is a child who is looked after by Veronica, who is not only an adoptive mother but also a foster carer. William looks on Thomas as a younger brother and he enjoys playing with him. He also said that he received visits from his uncle (his mother's brother) and

William's sketch

William Age 8
VRonica Age 33 mum
Iris   Age 63
Tomas Age 2
   Jack Age 85 dad
Uncle John

Karl
Josh
Mark

played with a cousin in the holidays.

This boy clearly enjoys active games and sports. He expressed some sadness about the fact that their flat had no garden, as he does not like sitting around watching TV. He also enjoys male company. Veronica has a friend called Jack who visits about once a week. William likes to identify him as 'Dad'. Sometimes Jack picks him up from school, he says, or takes him to play football in the park, and they exchange presents at birthdays. William thought that Jack was 85 years old, but he was somewhat hesitant about it and the interviewer felt that he might have got it wrong.

Unusually for children in this group, William was adopted as a very small baby. He came to live with his black adoptive parent within a month of his birth, and he came straight from the hospital with no experience of fostering. It was obvious that he felt safe and secure in his present mother's care, and he had no fears about being removed from the household. However, his understanding of adoption appeared to be affected by his knowledge of the fostering task undertaken by his mother. When asked what adoption 'meant', he said:

> *It's when you go to another family, and then when they can't have you as long as you want to, you have to go to a different one.*

He thought adoption would be a very difficult experience for anyone beyond babyhood, since they would feel sad about not seeing their friends. He had a good selection of young children's books about adoption, through which he was exploring these difficult issues.

William felt that he was no different from other children who have a Mum and a Dad in their house, but when he grew up he would marry, he said, and in that family there would be a Mum and a Dad. His children would have brothers and sisters as well as friends. He would also have a garden with trees and flowers.

Gail

Gail is a white girl aged 10. She came to live with her single adoptive mother about three years ago. Like many of the older children placed for adoption, she was accommodated for a long time in foster care; however, she was fortunate in having a good placement with a foster mother who prepared her well for adoption. She had been badly neglected in the past, and she had also suffered a mixture of physical and sexual abuse.

Gail liked the idea of constructing an "eco-map" as a way of portraying relationships, although she found the symbolism difficult to grasp at first. She tried a couple of experimental versions in which the names of her family members and friends floated free in small "bubbles" of space, none of which were touching each other. In the second version she grew more confident, varying the size of the bubbles to indicate the importance of the subjects; however, in this third version (which she prefaced by saying 'I've done it really wrong') the lines are heavier, the names more carefully delineated and the positions more strongly held. The biggest circle on the page represents her adoptive mother, Karen. She has placed a protective lifebelt around each person, but her own circle is pressed up against that of her mother, indicating her feeling of closeness.

Gail's drawing

Quite spontaneously, Gail said: 'I don't want a Dad – just a Mum. She does me fine.' Then she added: 'Not just any old Mum. *My* Mum.'

Gail presented as a very friendly, engaging girl with a pert sense of humour. She described her adoptive family as having 'about one thousand people in it', and this tallies with her mother's picture of a large extended family whose members met regularly for family functions. The central core, however, as far as Gail was concerned, was just her mother and herself. She was looking forward to the arrival of another adopted child, Amy. Amy's circle and the one representing Gail's birth sibling are both outlined in colour on the chart.

Contact with the birth family has not been maintained, although Gail thought she remembered saying goodbye to her birth mother a long time ago. Written contact is likely to be reinstated, perhaps with occasional meetings. In the meantime the adoptive mother and her daughter are happy in one another's company, and agree that they can enjoy shared activities such as swimming, walking or collecting things.

Karen, the adoptive mother, says that the child has 'a joie de vivre and a sparkiness that's good to have around'. For Gail, however, one of the biggest advantages of having one parent is still the fact that she 'doesn't have to have a horrible Dad'.

Suzanne

This nine-year-old black girl drew a portrait of her adoptive mother and herself and coloured it with felt pens. She drew with precision and attention to detail. The atmosphere is quiet and restrained, but also relaxed. Mother and daughter are at peace with one another.

One professional person who saw this picture commented on the fact that there was a space on the right of the page. Was there a missing person? The suggestion was made that Suzanne might want a father, or at least that she might want her mother to have a partner. However, the notes which were made at the time of the interview show that if there was a missing person, it was the birth mother.

When Suzanne began the drawing she said that she would 'put her other mother in'. She said that she would like to see her birth mother again, if it was possible. The trouble was that she lived a long way away.

I don't know if my Mum can drive there. You have to go on the motorway.

Overcoming her slight sadness, she said that her family now consisted of herself and her adoptive mother. By the time she had completed the second figure on the drawing, she had decided that there was no need to include any other person.

Suzanne had a good knowledge of her previous history, and also of her present family. She talked of her relatives in South America. She also mentioned the white family with whom she had been fostered for some time before the adoption. She had fond memories of this family, which had other children both older and younger than herself. There had been a dog, and an orchard where she took the dog for walks. She

Suzanne's drawing

Suzanne

could contact them if she wished, she said, but she scarcely remembers them now.

What was the reason for her adoption? Suzanne gave three reasons – firstly, the fact that her birth mother did not want her; secondly, the fact that she was a black person living with a white foster family; and thirdly, her adoptive mother had wanted a daughter.

Unlike many children in the sample, she made a clear distinction between fostering and adoption. For example, she said that you did not have to go to court if you were fostered, and she described the adoption hearing as being like 'getting married' (an apt description). However, she also saw the transition from fostering to adoption as being inevitably bound up with racial issues. 'When you are living with a white family,' she said, 'you have to get adopted to go somewhere else.'

She liked having a single Mum, she said, because it was peaceful and there were no headaches.

Lucy

Lucy is white and aged 13. She has been in her adoptive home for four years. The interviewer found her a chatty and active girl who exuded a lot of anxious energy. She asked a great many questions. However, she coped very bravely with the interview, which was a potentially difficult and threatening experience for her.

When asked to draw a picture of her family, Lucy enquired whether it should be 'this one or the other one'. Because she was given a free choice, she drew them both. At the top of the page she drew her birth family, which includes her previous parents and also brothers and sisters. Underneath and separated from the birth family by a strong crayoned line she depicted her adoptive mother and herself. The difference in the sizes and position of the figures is probably significant. In spite of the sadness of separation, Lucy's confidence in herself has increased since the adoption.

Lucy is now in telephone contact with some of her siblings, but not her parents. She explained that she goes to a 'special lady' (a

Lucy's drawing

counsellor or a therapist) to talk about some of the unpleasant things that happened at her old house. She does not usually speak of these things except to this lady or her adoptive mother. Both people have emphasised that none of the abuse she experienced was her fault, as at one time she was inclined to take the blame on herself.

The events which distressed her happened a long time ago, before she entered local authority care at the age of six. She had one spell in foster care followed by two successive placements in residential homes. She says that her memories of foster care are rather hazy, but it is clear that she expected the fostering placement to be permanent, and she was surprised when it ended.

From her conversation it was obvious that Lucy is extremely happy in her present home. She has had many stimulating and enjoyable experiences since the adoption, for example, learning to dance and play the flute, as well as Spanish lessons and visits to her adoptive mother's friends or members of the extended family. She talks a lot to her adoptive mother about all sorts of subjects. The most important thing, however, is that she knows this woman cares for her and loves her.

Lucy's other drawing

Lucy aged 13

Adoptive mum

At the time of the adoption, Lucy took great pleasure in choosing a new name for herself. When summarising her feelings about the adoption she said: 'I feel really happy with my Mum. I will be with her until the day I die.'

Maria

Maria is another white girl aged 13. Like Lucy, she came to her adoptive home about four years ago from a mixed background of fostering and children's homes. She had also been abused by other children while in residential care. Like Lucy, she decided to depict her birth family at the top of the page and her present family further down. However, her drawing has different qualities, and it is interesting that she refused to draw herself.

Animals are important to Maria. She cares devotedly for her cat and her two white rabbits, which are comically depicted in the drawing. Maria's somewhat jokey representation of her relatives and pets indicates her tremendous spirit and sense of humour, but it also belies the deep feeling she experiences when she thinks about her family. This feeling has expressed itself in her drawing of the birth mother. The woman's sensitive face is portrayed in profile as if it looks backwards into the past. The consultants from the Tavistock Clinic felt that the use of caricature, and also the absence of bodies in the drawing, may be protective devices to shield both the artist and the viewer against pain.

Maria has never known her birth father. She has had occasional contact with her birth mother, but not since she was placed for adoption. She says that she misses her 'loads'. She also misses her younger brother and her grandfather, whom she has seen more recently. At the same time she has an enormous respect and admiration for her adoptive mother, whom she describes as 'a saint'. She realises that she frequently pushes this woman to the limits of endurance in her release of anger but even when behaving badly, she knows and appreciates the fact that her adoptive mother cares.

Maria and her adoptive mother have had what she calls 'really nice times' as well. When our interviews were conducted, the girl was feeling the insecurity of her position as the plans for adoption had not

yet been finalised. Administrative slowness was adding to the burden of the waiting time. Maria had not been favourably impressed by the social workers she had met during her journeys through public care. She said that she had known at least four, and they had all abandoned her when she needed them most.

When the adoption is finalised, Maria would like to 'double-barrel' her surname. This would be a way of retaining her old family membership along with the new. She thinks that having one parent instead of two is not really important. 'Loads of people' at her school have only one parent. But when she grows up she will probably decide to adopt rather than to have children of her own, because she knows some of the pain which, on the road to adoption, many children have had to go through.

Nathan

This little black boy, who was adopted soon after birth, is six years old. He drew his picture quite purposefully and seemed happy in his adoptive family. He positioned himself not directly next to his adoptive mother but next to his maternal grandfather, who is liked and admired by him and obviously a significant male figure in his life. The maternal grandfather lives with the family and gives substantial help with child care. 'He picks me up after school,' said Nathan, 'and stays with me the rest of the day until Mummy comes home.'

Since Nathan was placed for adoption at a very young age and contact was discontinued, he has never known his birth family. He had been told that his birth mother was no more than a teenager when he was born. His view of adoption, quite reasonably, was: 'It's when somebody can't look after you, and they have to let someone else take care of you.' He thought this was a sensible idea, and he was pleased to have been chosen by his present mother.

Nathan's drawing

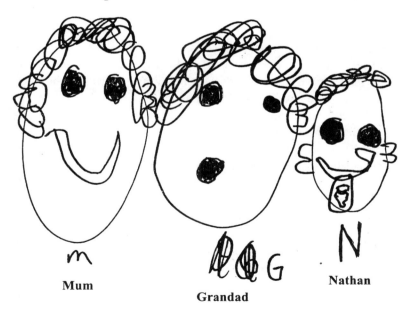

Mum

Grandad

Nathan

Both Nathan and his adoptive brother Rupert are children of mixed parentage; that is, they each have a black father and a white mother. The "racial" matching had obviously been carefully carried out by the adoption agency, since the adoptive mother herself had the same background. In part, this may have helped to cement the relationship between Nathan and his grandfather, who shares the ethnic origins of the child's own birth father. Certainly they appeared to be a close-knit family whose contact with the paternal relatives was strong and frequent.

Nathan takes pleasure in games and in school work, and he has many friends both black and white. He does not think there are any disadvantages associated with having only one parent.

When Nathan grows up he would like to be a sweet-maker, he said, specialising in chocolate and in chewits. He would like to have a lot of children, both natural and adopted. If given a choice of wishes-come-true he would prefer to win £50 million on the national lottery, to be a movie star and to live in the countryside, but he would not change his existing family, since he likes it 'just as it is'.

Jacqueline

Jacqueline is also aged six, and a black child – a small girl who appeared lively and enthusiastic. She talked proudly of her cultural heritage and of her real names, which were African and had been given to her by her black adoptive mother.

Mother and daughter clearly enjoyed going out and doing things together. Jacqueline said that she liked travelling on aeroplanes. They had been to Disneyland, to Tunisia and to Malta, she said, and she added almost in the same breath that they had recently been to netball (netball and aerobics were regular activities). She appeared to be a very sociable child who spoke warmly of her school-friends – mainly black children. She also showed a talented interest in music. When asked to draw her family, Jacqueline drew a large and vibrant family group containing a number of relatives.

Interestingly, Jacqueline drew herself twice in the picture. Her main self-portrait is positioned between her mother and her aunt, and coloured in red, but she depicted herself again on the extreme right,

Jacqueline's drawing

Sister

Mum

Aunty

Jacqueline

Aunt

Cousin

Uncle

next to her much younger adopted sister. In this second sketch she seems to have a role in supporting the other child. This interpretation is confirmed by her mother's descriptions of how well Jacqueline looks after her sister in everyday life.

From the drawing and from her conversation it appears that Jacqueline is capable of recognising herself in a number of different family roles. She relates to her aunts and uncles as a child among adults, introducing them with remarks such as 'This is Aunty x,' but in her explanation of family relationships it often seemed as though her primary relationship was with the child. For example, she would say, 'This is the mother of my cousin y'. Her understanding of the black family network, and her sense of involvement in it, was considerable.

For Jacqueline, a deep understanding of adoption was unnecessary. She knew the name of her birth mother and she also knew that she had lived with a foster family for the first few months of her life (she had photographs to prove it). However, she could not explain why she was adopted and she had no apparent understanding of what adoption meant. We had the impression that adoption was not a big issue in the household, and that some concepts had been filed quite safely and naturally for discussion at a later date, when Jacqueline's cognitive understanding and innate curiosity would lead the way in discovering them. In the meantime she was happy to be living in a large, warm and cohesive family, with a mother and a sister whom she described as 'great'.

Daniel

The drawing made by Daniel, who is a nine-year-old black boy, is different again from the others. We were struck by the comparative isolation of the figures, which are portrayed with thick brown trees separating the family members into segments of individual space. The level of interaction in the family does not seem to be high, as far as Daniel has experienced it, and yet there is a sense of order and privacy about the picture which is not unappealing. The figures are soundly based, with their feet on the ground. There is also evidence of a quirky sense of humour, for example, in the sunglasses and the arm muscles.

Daniel (in sunglasses)

Brother

Adoptive mum

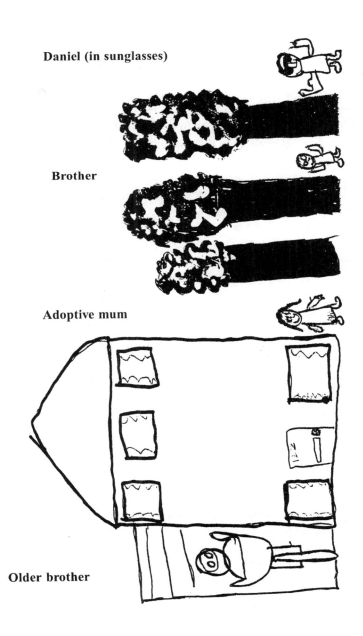

Older brother

Daniel's drawing

The interviews confirm that Daniel is "his own man".

It may be significant that the house is large and carefully drawn. Daniel and his family live in a council flat, with no garden and no car. At the time of the interviews they had already been moved once, out of a tower block and into their present accommodation, but they would shortly have to move again because the flat was only temporary. Daniel said that he would like to live in 'a rich house', and that he would also like to be able to buy a house for his adoptive mother.

Daniel was placed with his black adoptive mother at the age of fourteen months. At the time of his birth he was an extremely premature baby who was lucky to survive. He is a slow learner who admits to having difficulty with the work in school, but his mother recognises his achievements, and in her own interview she said:

> *He's made a tremendous effort to catch up. He's beginning to learn to read and write, which was very, very difficult for him at first . . . He has come a long way.*

Daniel does have friends of his own age whom he likes to see, and he also belongs to a youth club where he plays snooker and football. The leisure club is some distance away from the flat and he travels to it by bus. He says that he enjoys the activities. He does not play very much with his younger adopted brother, being very different from him in temperament, but he admires his older brother who is portrayed alongside the house in his cycling gear. This young man, who is the natural son of the adoptive mother, is in his early 20s. Daniel looks forward to his visits. He shows his admiration by copying the older boy's taste in clothes and in music.

No contact has taken place with Daniel's birth mother, and none is planned. His adoptive mother would answer questions if he requested it, but he has very little interest in adoption, and accepts that he is part of this family. When he grows up he would like to be a coach driver on school outings, he says, in addition to having a house and a family of his own.

Donna

Donna is white, and she is 13 years old. When she arrived in her adoptive home at the age of nine, it was her thirteenth move. She had been in and out of the care system for most of her childhood. Having been neglected in her birth family, she had been both sexually and physically abused in foster homes and in residential care.

The abuse which Donna had suffered was not fully disclosed until after the adoption. It had been impossible for her to talk about it at the time when it happened because there was no one close to her whom she felt she could trust. She had had a bad experience of social workers. As her experiences worsened, her behaviour became increasingly disturbed.

Donna now feels at home with her adoptive mother. She says that she can talk freely to this woman and that she gets on with her 'very well'. At the time of our interviews she had just been joined by two younger adopted sisters. She was progressing well at her special school, and enjoyed the company of other girls.

Donna drew two pictures, one after another. They have both been reproduced here because it is interesting to see the contrast between them. The first is a picture of the children's home where she used to live. There are four little faces, belonging to children whom Donna previously regarded as her friends, peering out of a solitary attic window. The house is oddly shaped, and vaguely institutional in design (the bars are reminiscent of a prison or the front of a military uniform, but the doors are those of a hospital ward). The figure on the left, out in the cold, is the birth mother. On the right of the picture is the birth mother's new baby. This large and bouncy child is clearly doing very well, and in fact she is the only person in the picture who seems to be prospering.

In the second picture Donna has been adopted. The house represents their adoptive home but the family members have come out of it and are romping around in the garden. The house itself is more normal in design, with a gently smoking chimney (perhaps representing warmth and expression of feeling), whilst there is a number on the door to enable other people to find it. The heavy sky has gone. The Tavistock Clinic consultants who saw this picture were unanimous in

Donna's drawing

Donna's other drawing

saying that it was happier and healthier than the previous one.

Like the other children who had been interviewed, Donna had been generous in admitting us to the privacy of her memories. When she had had enough of questions she said, 'That's it, the end,' and in celebration of her perfect right to end the interview, she turned off the tape recorder herself.

15 Placement outcomes

Inasmuch as none of the placements studied had broken down, they can all be regarded as successful. However, some were more successful than others, in the sense that children in these placements were developing extremely well and there was a strong feeling of shared satisfaction with the adoption.

In this section we shall gather together some of the evidence gained from file studies and interviews and relate it to the information obtained from the Assessment and Action Records (AARs) of the Looking After Children (LAC) schedules. As reported in Chapter 4, these schedules were designed to measure the outcomes of parenting for children across seven dimensions: health, education, identity, family and social relationships, social presentation, emotional and behavioural development, and self-care skills.

The AARs were completed during the final interview, with the aid of much detailed discussion involving the adoptive parents and sometimes older children. In this way systematic information was obtained about the children's progress. This information is the best evidence we have of the "outcome" of the adoptions at the point when final interviews were conducted.

To present this material fairly, we have to take into account the starting points of the children. All of the children had special needs. Accordingly it makes sense to look separately at the quality of care provided by the adopters and the extent of the children's progress, using the customary distinction between "service" and "welfare" outcomes. When dealing with welfare outcomes, also, we must try to avoid discriminating unfairly against children who were physically disabled or had learning difficulties.

Service outcomes: what the adopters provided
When we look back to the referrals from the local authorities, we realise that severe medical or educational problems were almost always known

through the assessments conducted at or around the time of the placement, and that most of these identified needs were given prompt attention by the adopters during the post-placement period. Squints and other remediable defects noted on the files had been corrected, and several children had had speech therapy. However, the involvement of the adopters went beyond the provision of routine services. Some of the single parents with special medical skills or experience achieved quite remarkable results. The recovery of the power of hearing for a previously deaf and blind child, mentioned in Chapter 9, is one example. Another is the use of skin-grafting to remove the traces of physical injuries originally suffered by a young girl in child abuse. The scars which embarrassed her when she had to undress in the swimming pool, and which had previously been regarded as untreatable, are no longer visible.

As far as parenting input was concerned, the entries on the LAC schedules show that the adoptive parents were conscientious. They took their children to the dentist regularly, attended to immunisations, and saw to it that they received an adequate diet. The diet of the adopted children is actually better than average, although like other factors this is probably associated with higher income and a slightly better standard of living. Accident prevention was good. All but one of the children in the 5–9 age range were protected by having medicines, cleaning fluids and poisonous substances kept out of reach. Fires were adequately protected with guards, which were considered more essential for disabled children than for the others.

The schedule material indicates that progress in education was helped by the provision of a safe, encouraging and stimulating environment, together with a close liaison between home and school. The adopters were constantly negotiating with officialdom on behalf of their children. Where necessary the child was helped by "statementing" which led to the provision of welfare assistance in the classroom or special schooling, and in a few cases the parents paid for home tuition. One mother taught the child herself when he was excluded from school.

Much was achieved simply through building up the children's confidence. However, when children were a long way behind their contemporaries it was obviously difficult for them to catch up, and their school work was sometimes impeded by chronic difficulties. Ten of the children (21 per cent of the sample) had learning disabilities, and almost half the sample had some degree of learning difficulty. Consequently the average educational performance in the adoptive sample was low, even though there were some high-achieving children and the disabled children often had special skills.

From the time of the adoption, or more accurately from the time of the placement, the adoptive parents fostered a sense of identity by providing continuous care for the children. However, they were only too conscious of the disruption which the children had experienced previously, in the birth family or the care system, and felt that in many cases it would be difficult for them to make good this deficit. In particular, they were critical of the extent to which records had been lost and family histories allowed to recede into oblivion. They wanted more information about the past, so that they could nurture the child's sense of identity by making necessary links to the present.

The need for continuity in the lives of some of the adopted children was very apparent. One of the questions asked in the LAC schedules was:

> *How many times has the child's household changed in a way that has meant that a new person has looked after him or her?*

In a sample of children adopted from the care system two such changes might be expected, but 78 per cent of children in the 10–15 age group had had more than three such changes, and 43 per cent had experienced a new carer between five and 14 times. About half the children in both the main age groups (that is, between five and 15) had also experienced at least one unscheduled change of school.

This rate of discontinuity suggests that the number of previous admissions to local authority accommodation was higher for these children than for the adoptees studied by Murch *et al* in 1991, and of course it leaves out of account the number of times children had moved from home to hospital and back again, or had spent short stays with relatives while the same carer remained in charge.

Another question which related to the sense of identity as well as to the maintenance of family and social relationships was: Has the child had continuing contact with at least one adult throughout his or her life?

A positive answer was given for only 43 per cent of five to nine-year-olds and 22 per cent of those between 10 and 15.

One method of ensuring continuity for late-placed children was, of course, to arrange ongoing contact with members of the birth family at the time when the child was placed for adoption. Table 14 in Chapter 13 shows the results of these arrangements, as far as face-to-face contact was concerned. In spite of the difficulties recorded in Chapter 13, the incidence of such contact was actually quite high when compared with the data from other studies (Fratter *et al*, 1991; Department of Health, 1995). Sixteen children out of 48 (one-third of the sample) had face-to-face contact with one or more members of their birth family, and in most recent adoptions there was some exchange of letters. Ethnicity was sometimes considered (wrongly) to be a matter for black children only, but both black and white adopters ensured that children were clear about their cultural and ethnic origins.

Did the single status of the parent have any discernible effect on community participation? The LAC schedule responses show that over half the adopted children in the 10–15 age group were encouraged to take part in organised physical activity. The children in the adoptive sample were also frequent attenders at social clubs. A smaller proportion attended after-school clubs which involved intellectual pursuits such as chess or computers, but this finding has to be seen in the context of children's learning difficulties.

The central core of adoption is, of course, the parent–child relationship. The content of the interviews and our own observations suggest that the quality of the relationship between the children and the adoptive parents was usually extremely good, and this is confirmed by the data from the LAC schedules. Ninety-three per cent of the adopted children between the ages of five and nine, and 70 per cent of those aged 10 to 15, were apparently shown physical affection 'often' by their adoptive parents. When children in the 10 to 15 age group were asked how well they got on with their adoptive parents, the answer was 'very well' in 87 per cent of cases and 'no obvious problems' in a further nine per cent. The parents agreed with this judgement in over 90 per cent of cases.

Welfare outcomes: the progress made by the children

In the version of the AARs which was used in the research, there were two or three summary statements at the end of each section in which the parent was invited to rate the child's progress on a scale between nought and 50. These judgements are of necessity somewhat arbitrary; however, since they were made after detailed discussion and consideration of the relevant issues, and since the parents were generally anxious to estimate children's progress accurately in order to improve their own parenting skills, it seems reasonable to believe that when these scores are aggregated they will provide some tangible evidence of progress within the group.

In order to preserve a balance between the outcome dimensions when the scores were aggregated, and at the same time rule out certain specific areas of progress such as success in school examinations which would have discriminated unfairly against children with Down's Syndrome, only one key summary statement was chosen from each of six dimensions. (Self-care was excluded entirely.) The list of key statements is as follows:

1. The child is normally well and thriving in growth and development.
2. The child is acquiring special skills and interests.
3. The child has positive self-esteem.
4. The child has close emotional ties with at least one caregiver.
5. The child's appearance and behaviour are acceptable to peers and adults.
6. The child is free of serious emotional and behavioural problems.

When the accumulated responses to these statements were considered, three groups were identified: firstly, a group of 12 children who represented the most successful adoptions at the time when interviews were conducted; secondly, an intermediate group of 24 children with mixed scores; and thirdly, a group of 12 children who had made less progress than the others. The results of this exercise must be treated with care. However, some interesting patterns have been obtained, and some very basic research questions can now be asked and answered.

Which were the most successful adoptions?

The 12 children who head the list of aggregated scores – that is, the top 25 per cent of the sample in terms of current progress – are mainly young children but they contain representatives of every age group in the research. Four children were aged between three and four years at the time when our interviews were conducted and three children were between five and nine; but there were also four children between the ages of 10 and 15 and one aged over 16.

In terms of special needs, one child in this group was physically disabled and another had Down's Syndrome. Three of the adolescents were white children who had come from deprived backgrounds and had previously exhibited problems but who were now in stable placements.

The children referred to above were all being given patient, skilled and sensitive care and were making excellent progress, but it is particularly noticeable that eight of the 12 children in this top-scoring group are black. (Five of them were African or African-Caribbean and three were of mixed parentage.) This means that half the black children in the total sample appear in the top 25 per cent of results if our outcome measures can be relied on. A further check shows that the remaining children who were black or of mixed parentage are mostly in the next quarter-segment down, which means that their developmental record still places them in the upper half of the sample.

The good progress of the black children – and particularly their high ratings on attachment and self-esteem – might seem to indicate that the "same-race" matching policies of the adoption agencies were justified. Certainly credit must be given for the care and skill with which the matching was done. However, as previously mentioned, we have no data on transracial adoptions which could provide a comparison group, and there are also other factors which must have contributed to a good outcome in these particular cases. Firstly, the black children were younger than the others: four in this group were aged between three and four, and another three between five and nine at the time of the interviews. Secondly, they entered their placements early: five of these children were placed in their adoptive families during their first year of life, and the others had all been placed by the age of six. It should be emphasised also that there were outstanding successes among the older white children in this top 25 per cent of the sample, in spite of reports of extensive disruption during the early years. Some of these adoptions were long established, and the children were well settled in their adoptive families.

The attitudes of all the adopters, both black and white, were extremely positive. The children enjoyed living in multiracial communities and mixing with children of different backgrounds including their own.

Which adoptions were least successful?

Once again, a number of age groups are represented among the 12 children who seemed to be progressing least well at the time when our interviews were conducted (though it has to be remembered that this is a relative measure). These children were generally older than the ones in the top scoring group. Two were aged over 16, eight were between the ages of 10 and 15, and two were aged five to nine. They were all white, and there were no children in this group under the age of five.

Figure 2 shows the contrast between the most successful and the least successful adoptions in terms of mean scores, and it also includes the scores of the intermediate group. It will be seen that the differences are not constant on each dimension. The children in the least successful group had been given reasonably good ratings on physical health and development and (with a very few exceptions) on attachment to the carer, but they had lower scores on self-esteem and emotional/behavioural development – often below the halfway mark, which many parents saw as significant. They also scored relatively low on the acquisition of skills and interests and social acceptability.

The timing of the interviews clearly had an effect. Five of these children had been placed for less than two years, and in two cases the placement was less than six months in duration. Quite understandably, the prospective adoptive parents in these cases reported a high rate of disturbance and a low rate of attachment, since the children were still in a relatively strange environment and they had not had time to bond fully with their carers. It may be assumed that these recently placed children were probably going through a stage of temporary problems which would diminish in time. However, the other seven children had all been placed for a considerable period, which was not less than four years and in two

175

cases more than ten years. In some of these long-standing adoptions there were persistent problems which were regarded as endemic, although the carers' commitment to the children remained unabated and they were also capable of deriving satisfaction from the adoptions.

Further investigation reveals that all the children in this low-achieving group had learning difficulties, although only three could be classed as having learning disabilities. (It is interesting to note that the children in the sample who were described as having Down's Syndrome showed a great deal of variety, especially in self-esteem and emotional/behavioural development, and their scores were evenly spread throughout the whole sequence of results.)

We do not know how far the learning difficulties we recorded were genetic, and how far they were the result of developmental delay because of abuse or neglect in the birth family or the care system. However, it is clear that in some cases these difficulties were associated with slightly lowered performance right across the range of dimensions in the schedules. As is well known, lack of success in the school system can lead to isolation from the peer group, and it is also associated with low acquisition of skills and interests, but these children's sense of identity, and in some cases their degree of attachment, could have been affected by their inability to understand the discontinuity with which they had been treated. Minor but persistent behaviour problems also led to a low rate of social acceptability, and the children's self-esteem was not enhanced. In spite of these difficulties, however, the average level of attachment to the single carer remained high.

Nine of these 12 children had a known history of physical or sexual abuse (sometimes both) and in one other case abuse was suspected but could not be confirmed. One adolescent girl had previously received therapeutic counselling and for four other children treatment had been arranged or was actually in progress. For the five remaining children whose difficult behaviour may have been abuse related, no treatment had yet been offered.

It should be emphasised that these broad differences within the sample become less significant when we consider the detailed picture. Figure 3 charts the pattern of results for the three groups of children who, as we originally noted, were selected for adoption by single people: firstly, the black children with cultural needs; secondly, the children who were physically disabled or had learning disabilities; and thirdly, those who had been abused or neglected in the birth family. The ups and downs on this chart represent the accumulated strengths and weaknesses of these children, as they strove to cope with life in the aftermath of the adoption.

What does all this say about the adopters?

It may seem surprising that in the face of considerable problems many of the single carers were still expressing strong commitment to the children at the time of our interviews, and they were also capable of deriving satisfaction from the adoptions. For some adoptive parents, the rewards came from being needed, but they had respect as well as sympathy and affection for the children, being aware of the previous events which had contributed to their difficulties and understanding the reasons why certain coping strategies had been chosen. There were only a very few cases where help might perhaps have been offered at an earlier stage, to

Figure 2

Progress of all children at the point when interviews were conducted (Mean scores on a scale between 0 and 50)

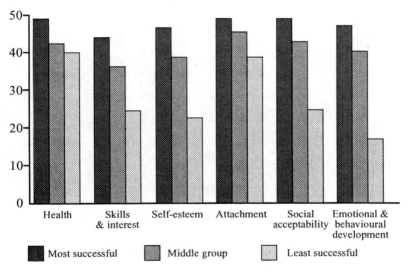

avoid the build-up of chronic problems.

The three groups whom we identified as "novices", "old hands" and "professionals" are represented throughout the sequence of results we have just outlined. When matched with suitable children, they were all bringing to the adoptions their own particular mixture of warmth, persistence and skill. There were occasional difficulties which seemed to stem from a slight mismatch of child and parent, but the same difficulties might have been expected to occur in so-called "ordinary" families. The difference in the children's outcomes appears to be mainly due to factors which are not connected with single parenting, that is, the age of the children, their age at placement, the length of time they had spent in their new families and the degree of pre-placement adversity.

The adopters realised and accepted their children's disabilities. However, they were also convinced that without their committed and determined input, progress for some of the children could have been very much worse.

Figure 3

Progress of all children according to special needs (Mean scores on a scale between 0 and 50)

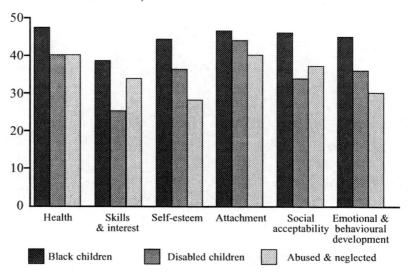

Summary

- The entries on the LAC schedules show that the single adopters were conscientious. They took necessary action to meet the children's social needs, as well as their needs in health and education, and generally did everything possible to further their mental and physical welfare.

- The adoptive parents fostered a sense of identity by providing continuous care for the children. This was very much needed, since some children had experienced an unusual degree of disruption in the birth family and the care system.

- Eight of the 12 children in the top-scoring group were black. These children were younger than the others and had entered their placements at an earlier age. They had settled well with single black carers.

- In the least successful group there were several children who had been placed recently, and who were clearly undergoing temporary problems. However, all the children in the low-achieving group had learning difficulties, and nine of the 12 children had a known history of physical or sexual abuse. For five of these children, no treatment had been offered.

- In spite of ongoing difficulties in some cases, the adopters still expressed strong commitment to the children and were capable of finding the adoptions rewarding. The level of attachment was high.

- No significant differences were noted in the progress scores of children adopted by the "novices", the "old hands" and the "professionals". All of these people were capable of performing well, when matched with children who suited their skills and previous experience. The main limiting factors in terms of outcome seemed to be the age of the children, their age at placement, the length of time they had spent in their new families and the degree of pre-placement adversity.

16 Implications for policy and practice

When the implications of this research are considered, it is useful to remember that a recent study of adoption services in three local authorities has confirmed the urgent need for adoptive placements (Department of Health, 1993b). The members of the Social Services Inspectorate who carried out this study found that in the two local authorities for which reliable information was available,

> . . . *a significant number of children had been awaiting placement for over a year, and a smaller but no less significant number for over two years.*

Fewer than half of these children were healthy babies made available with parental agreement. The remainder were children with special needs, or children who were looked after by the local authority without any prospect of rehabilitation. The authorities' success in finding suitable placements decreased in relation to the child's age above five years.

Policy implications

Given the needs of children currently in the care system, the demand for adoptive parents with particular skills is clearly acute. Our study suggests that many single people have the necessary ability, together with time, energy and commitment, but the lack of information about the requirements or discriminatory treatment at various stages in the adoption process, can make them feel "less eligible" than couples. In the initial stages this feeling deters suitable people from applying. When experienced later, it can undermine the adopters' confidence in their parenting. There is a clear need to improve information and ease of access if the skills of single people – both men and women – are to be used in adoption.

Single people are potentially a flexible as well as talented resource.

The study revealed some interesting ways of involving single applicants both in adoption and in the activity of supporting one another, such as the arrangements for single people to parent individual members of a sibling group, as described in Chapter 6. The movement towards a greater involvement of developmental psychologists in assessment, together with awareness of demographic changes and a focus on outcome in recent research, have probably been instrumental in shifting professional opinion away from undue reliance on family stereotypes and concentrating attention on the parent–child relationship. As a result, single carers seem to have been deliberately targeted in certain cases because of the specific skills which they had to offer. (This happened particularly in the fields of health and social care.) However, in the actual search for families, as the records show, two parents have often been required as a first choice by the local authorities. The resulting delay in finding placements has probably been damaging to children's interests.

Messages for the selection of adopters

Fears have been expressed about the possible vulnerability of children because of the "difference" of single-person adoption. However, the interviews with children who had been adopted by single carers show that they did not feel unusual and they certainly did not feel stigmatised by belonging to a single parent family (see Chapter 14). Many children had known only one parent in the birth family. Both the adoptive parents and the children experienced their family structure as normal. Feelings of difference, where they existed, were associated with the adoption itself and the events which had preceded it. These feelings were acknowledged and dealt with sensitively by the adopters.

The study uncovered many positive features of single-person adoption. Consistency of parenting was relatively easy to achieve, and decision-making was often simpler than it would have been in a two-parent family. Relationships with young children were sometimes quite intense, but as the North American research also noted, this intensity could be helpful in stimulating attachment. The families were outward looking because of the adopters' involvement in employment and community activities.

As far as the assessment processes are concerned, the study underlines the need for anti-discriminatory treatment in group meetings and workshops. In these situations, which were almost always perceived as slightly threatening, single people sometimes felt at a disadvantage compared with people who were married or cohabiting, especially if there were individual differences of age, sex and ethnicity. Careful questioning is obviously necessary to ensure that all possible problems have been anticipated; but we need to ask whether it is right for the hurdles to be set at a higher level for single people, and for the regulations to be more rigidly enforced. Where this is not the case, reassurances need to be given, so that the single applicants can relax and profit from the learning experience as well as drawing strength from the group (Thorpe *et al*, 1993).

Throughout the study it was apparent that assessments which focused too exclusively on the single status of the applicant were likely to be misguided for a number of reasons.

Firstly, *it was important to recognise the extent of diversity among the adopters*. The single people came from a variety of backgrounds, not simply in terms of marital status but in terms of skills and life-experiences. It is a mistake to regard single adopters, or their children, as a homogeneous group.

Secondly, *research findings about single parents in general cannot readily be applied to single adopters*. The parents in the study had always made a deliberate decision to parent a child. For many other single parents, pregnancy is unplanned and sometimes unwelcome (Burghes and Brown, 1995).

Thirdly, *assessments which focused too exclusively on the single status of the adopter were in danger of obscuring other information of importance*. For example, the problem from the past which was most difficult for some single adoptive applicants to resolve, and which could interfere with the ready establishment of a good relationship with the adopted child, was not the experience of broken partnership or the absence of a partner, it was the experience of infertility (see also Brebner *et al*, 1985).

There are, of course, some caveats about the selection of single adoptive parents which are relevant, and which need to be carefully considered. One is at least partly recognised already. It is that single adopters need an exceptionally good social support system in order to avoid problems of social isolation. However, the adopters in the study were well supported by friends and associates as well as members of the extended family. Secondly, they needed to be confident in their own ability to parent as a single person. In terms of family changes, the arrival of new adopted siblings could be coped with and was generally beneficial to the family, but there were risks involved in forming a new partnership after the adoption, especially if a single woman took a husband because she felt anxious about parenting on her own. Paradoxically, a woman might well feel obliged to do this if she felt under pressure from the two-parent ideology which is inherent in current legislation and policy, but the more competent adopters were able to separate the tasks of partnership and of parenting, and to recognise (and value) the tasks in which they were involved.

Preparation and training
The single adopters did not find that all children who were defined as having "special needs" were equally difficult to parent. Young black children who had been placed for cultural reasons proved to be very rewarding and made excellent progress with single black carers, who provided them with a helpful narrative to explain the adoption. A high degree of personal satisfaction was also reported by people who had adopted children with physical or learning disabilities. In spite of the work which was involved in caring for these exceptionally dependent children, it seemed that they often gave back as much as they received. The feeling of being valued by the community was part of this picture.

Gender was a frequent topic for discussion in the research interviews. Some adopters worried about its implications, especially where a single woman had adopted a boy who was growing into manhood, even if there was a plentiful supply of role models. In most cases the women appeared to be worrying unnecessarily, as a result of social pressures. There was no indication that boys adopted by single women were progressing badly. However, some children with special needs were happy to be living with a carer of the same gender. This applied particularly to girls who had been sexually abused, many of whom felt healed and protected by living with a single mother. It also applied to two boys with traditional "male" interests who were living with single fathers. In these cases they valued the presence of a boisterous adult who shared their interests. For both boys and girls, however, the adoptions held out the hope that attitudes would become modified over time, as children left behind the negative effects of earlier experiences and developed a more balanced approach to gender roles.

Ethnicity, gender and disability were all fertile topics for discussion in relation to single-person adoption. At present gender appears to have a lower priority than ethnicity, and in view of the adopters' anxieties it is possible that a realignment of priorities needs to take place. However, the most severe problems, and the situations which were most emotionally "draining", were faced by people who adopted late-placed children with emotional or behavioural difficulties. It was useful and sometimes essential for these adopters to be able to talk to other adoptive parents, whether married or single – partly for companionship or sympathy, and partly to learn (and to revise continually) what it might be reasonable to expect of them or their children. Commitment or a liking for young people was not enough. The most important part of the preparatory work in these cases was to develop sensitive understanding of children's difficulties.

Chapter 7 outlines three groups of adopters whom we have called the "novices", the "old hands" and the "professionals". Each of these groups had strengths and weaknesses related to their previous experience and it was important to get the matching right. However, one of the main determinants of outcome appeared to be the children's pre-existing disabilities, where these existed, and in some cases it might have been useful for the adopters to predict, but not be confined by, the likely limits of children's progress (see Figures 2 and 3 in Chapter 15).

Figure 2 compares the most successful with the least successful adoptions, as well as those in between, and it shows where the deficits occurred. It may be seen as predictable that the greatest contrasts between the first group and the third are in the realm of emotional and behavioural development. However, the interviews and the material presented in Figure 3 show that lack of progress on one dimension could to some extent be compensated for by other successes. For example, extremely naughty children could still be physically healthy and socially acceptable, and the adopter could derive satisfaction from the development of skills and interests. Even where children were severely disabled, too, the rewards could be considerable because of the level of attachment to the carer. The analysis also forces us to think about the necessary balance and the relationship between the outcome dimensions. In the case of disabled children the adopters found it most difficult to develop skills and interests, but for previously abused and neglected children, the biggest problem was the maintenance of self-esteem.

The great strength of the adoptions by single carers was the level of attachment offered. This helped them to understand vulnerable children and to relate well to them, but they were constantly having to devise new strategies to deal with learning difficulties, and to maintain children's fluctuating self-esteem through the various stages of childhood. In some cases, too, they needed help to prevent the disabled children from becoming unduly dependent.

In the case of older children, there is disturbing evidence that single adopters may have been asked to cope with children who had suffered an unusual degree of pre-placement adversity. This confirms our impression that single people are regarded by the local authorities as "less eligible" to adopt, and that one aspect of this lower eligibility may be discriminatory treatment in the allocation of children; this makes their achievements all the more remarkable when we reflect on improvements over time. Even "professional" adopters saw themselves as mothers or fathers rather than officially sanctioned carers, and it was important to them in the beginning that the right relationship should be established and maintained. (One adopter of five disabled children said: 'People think I'm running a children's home; but this is my *family*'.)

Needed resources
As far as service provision is concerned, the study supports the need for continuing partnership between the statutory and voluntary sectors, and the preservation of relationships, if possible, between the family and particular workers whom they have learned to trust. Ongoing training or consultancy, together with easy access to specialised therapeutic services (for example, art or play therapy, or counselling) might have been of benefit to some of the adopters of abused and neglected children, and

there is no doubt that such facilities should be regularly available. In some cases, too, the adopters may need encouragement to make use of them. However, the main needs of the single adopters we interviewed were often for time and money. They needed a reasonable period of adoption leave at the time when the child was placed, and sufficient income to help them to provide a good quality of life for the child (Hill *et al*, 1989; Rhodes, 1993). Adoption leave and adoption allowances were not a luxury. In most cases they were a necessity, and it was helpful if they had been negotiated at the time when a placement was made.

General conclusions
There are four clear points emerging from the study, which may contribute to the continuing debate about family structure in adoption policy and practice.
1. Single people deserve to be given special help so that they will not feel "less eligible" as adopters. Given the needs of the children currently in the public care system and awaiting permanent placements, single people with the necessary skills are often uniquely equipped to parent them.
2. It makes sense for adoption agencies and local authorities to develop ways of assessing potential parents on a mixture of caring skills and social supports. Marital or partnership structure is important, but only as one factor among many. Sibling structures, which are largely within the control of single adopters, also have an impact.
3. The experiences of black single adopters and their children are different from those of white people. In general there are more hurdles for black adoptive parents to overcome. Continuous positive action may be necessary to encourage recruitment and to support these placements.
4. Single-person adoption has many advantages, but it seems to be particularly indicated in the following circumstances:
    (i) where there is a need for a permanent carer with an unusual degree of commitment and skill, gained from life experiences including time spent in employment;
    (ii) where it is advisable for a child to have all the benefits of a close, one-to-one relationship with a single parent, in a situation

which does not place too much pressure on either of them;

(iii) where it is helpful to be able to select the gender of the carer (whether this is male or female); and

(iv) where circumstances suggest that other children in the household will also have adopted status, to avoid problems of conflict between natural and adopted children.

One final point needs to be made. Prospective adopters who are single should not be limited by being considered only for children with special needs. In some cases they may be highly suited to the adoption of "ordinary" children, and if they are not to be treated as a partially disqualified group, they need to be assessed and offered opportunities in the same way as everyone else. By acknowledging their special skills and commitment, however, we shall give them some of the credit they deserve, and we may also support their efforts to implement, in their own contact with children and birth families, the positive aspects of the principle which has been described as "acknowledgement of difference".

References

Adcock M, Kaniuk J and White R, *Exploring Openness in Adoption*, Significant Publications, 1993.

Ahmed S, Cheetham J and Small J, *Social Work with Black Children and their Families*, BAAF/Batsford, 1986.

Anderson M, 'The relevance of family history,' in Anderson M (ed) *Sociology of the Family: Readings*, Penguin, 1980.

Anderson M, 'The social implications of demographic change', in Thompson F M L (ed) *The Cambridge Social History of Britain*, Vol. 2, Cambridge University Press, 1990.

Barth R P and Berry M, *Adoption and Disruption: Rates, risks and responses*, Aldine de Gruyter, USA, 1988.

Bean P, *Adoption: Essays in social policy, law and sociology*, Tavistock Publications, ed. 1984.

Beresford B, *Expert Opinions: A national survey of parents caring for a severely disabled child*, The Policy Press, 1995.

Berger B, 'The bourgeois family and modern society', in Davies J (ed) *The Family: Is it just another lifestyle choice?*, ILEA Health and Welfare Unit, London, 1993.

Berridge D and Cleaver H, *Foster Home Breakdown*, Blackwell, 1987.

Bevan H K, 'The role of the court in the adoption process', In Bean P (ed) *Adoption: Essays in Social Policy, Law and Sociology*, 1984.

Bilge B and Kaufman G, 'Children of divorce and one-parent families: cross-cultural perspectives', *Family Relations*, 32, pp. 59–71, 1983.

Borland M, O'Hara G and Triseliotis J, 'Placement outcomes for children with special needs,' *Adoption & Fostering*, 15:2, pp. 18–28, 1991.

Boswell J, *The Kindness of Strangers*, Penguin, 1988.

Bradshaw J and Millar J, *Lone Parent Families in the UK* Department of Social Security Research Report No. 6, HMSO, 1991.

Bradshaw J and Millar J, 'Lone mothers: family employment and benefit changes', *Benefits*, 9, 1994.

Branham E, 'One Parent Adoptions', *Children*, 17:103–07, 1970.

Brebner C M, Sharp J D and Stone F H, *The Role of Infertility in Adoption*, BAAF, 1985.

British Agencies for Adoption & Fostering, *The BAAF Response to the Review of Adoption Law*, BAAF, 1993.

Brodzinsky D M and Schechter M D, *The Psychology of Adoption*, Oxford University Press, 1990.

Brodzinsky D M, Schechter D E and Brodzinsky A B, 'Children's knowledge of adoption: developmental changes and implications for adjustment', in Ashmore R and Brodzinsky D (eds), *Thinking about the Family: Views of parents and children*, Erlbaum, USA, 1986.

Brown H C, 'Competent child-focused practice: working with lesbian and gay carers', *Adoption & Fostering*, 15:2, pp. 11–17, 1991.

Burghes L, *Lone Parenthood and Family Disruption: The outcomes for children*, Occasional Paper 18, Family Policy Studies Centre, 1994.

Burghes L and Brown M, *Single Lone Mothers: Problems, prospects and policies*, Family Policy Studies Centre, 1995.

Caine H, *What Sort of Family? Experiences of placing children with non-traditional families,* Barnardo's, 1990.

Case C and Dalley T, *Working with Children in Art Therapy*, Routledge, 1990.

Cattanach A, *Play Therapy with Abused Children*, Jessica Kingsley, 1992.

Cleaver H and Freeman P, *Parental Perspectives in Cases of Suspected Child Abuse*, HMSO, 1995.

Clulow C and Mattinson J, *Marriage Inside Out: Understanding problems of intimacy*, Penguin, 1989.

Cowan C P and Cowan P A, *When Partners become Parents: The big life change for couples*, Basic Books, USA, 1992.

Cullen D, *Response to the Draft Adoption Bill*, BAAF, 1996.

Dallos R, *Family Belief Systems, Therapy and Change*, Open University Press, 1991.

Daly K, 'Parenthood as problematic' in Gilgun *et al*, *Qualitative Methods in Family Research*, Sage Publications, 1992.

Dance C, *Focus on Adoption: A snapshot of adoption patterns in England – 1995*, BAAF, 1997.

Davies J, *The Family: Is it just another lifestyle choice?*, ILEA Health and Welfare Unit, London, ed 1993.

Department of Health, *The Children Act 1989: Guidance and Regulations. Volume 9, Adoption issues*, HMSO, 1991.

Department of Health and Welsh Office, *Review of Adoption Law*, Report to Ministers of an Interdepartmental Working Group, 1992.

Department of Health and Welsh Office, *Adoption: The future*, White Paper, HMSO, 1993.

Department of Health, *Planning for Permanence? Adoption Services in Three Northern Local Authorities*, Report by the Social Services Inspectorate, 1993b.

Department of Health, *Moving Goalposts: A study of post-adoption contact in the North of England*, Report by the Social Services Inspectorate, 1995.

Department of Health and Welsh Office, *Adoption – A service for children*, A consultative document on the Adoption Bill, 1996.

Dickerson B J, *African American Single Mothers*, Sage Publications, 1995.

Dornbusch S M *et al*, 'Single Parents, Extended households and the control of adolescents', *Child Development*, 56, pp. 326–41, 1985.

Dougherty S, 'Single adoptive parents and their children', in *Social Work*, 23, pp. 311–14, 1978.

Dunn J, *Sisters and Brothers*, Fontana, 1984.

Dunn J, *Young Children's Close Relationships: Beyond Attachment*, Sage Publications, 1993.

Dwivedi K N and Varma V P, *Meeting the Needs of Ethnic Minority Children*. Jessica Kingsley, 1996.

190

Erikson E H, *Identity: Youth and crisis*, Norton, USA, 1968.

Fahlberg V I, *A Child's Journey through Placement*, UK edition, BAAF, 1994.

Farmer E and Owen M, *Child Protection Practice: Private risks and public remedies*, HMSO, 1995.

Feigelman W and Silverman A R, 'Single-parent adoptions', *Social Casework*, 58, pp. 418–425, 1977.

Finch J and Mason J, *Negotiating Family Responsibilities*, Tavistock/Routledge, 1993.

Firth R, Hubert J and Forge A, *Families and their Relatives*, Routledge & Kegan Paul, 1970.

Fratter J, *Family Placement and Access: Achieving permanency for children in contact with birth parents*, Barnardo's, 1989.

Fratter J, Rowe J, Sapsford D and Thoburn J, *Permanent Family Placement: A decade of experience*, BAAF, 1991.

Gaber I and Aldridge J, *In the Best Interests of the Child: Culture, identity and transracial adoption*, Free Association Books, eds 1994.

George V, *Foster Care: Theory and practice*, Routledge & Kegan Paul, 1970.

Gill O and Jackson B, *Adoption and Race*, Batsford, 1983.

Glennerster H, *British Social Policy since 1945*, Blackwell, 1995.

Goffman E, *Stigma: Notes on the management of spoiled identity*, Prentice Hall, 1963, reprinted Penguin 1990.

Goodacre I, *Adoption Policy and Practice*, Allen & Unwin, 1966.

Gordon T, *Feminist Mothers*, Macmillan, 1990.

Gottman J S, 'Children of gay and lesbian parents', *Marriage and Family Review*, 14:3–4, pp. 176–96, 1989.

Green M D, Mandel J B, Hotvedt M E, Gray J and Smith L, 'Lesbian mothers and their children: a comparison with solo parent heterosexual mothers and their children', *Archives of Sexual Behaviour*, 15:2, pp. 167–84, 1986.

Green R G and Crooks P D, 'Family member adjustment and family dynamics in established single-parent and two-parent families', *Social Service Review*, 62, pp.600–13, 1988.

Grieve R and Hughes M, *Understanding Children*, Blackwell, eds 1990.

Groze V K and Rosenthal J A, 'Single parents and their adopted children: A psychosocial analysis', *Families in Society: The Journal of Contemporary Human Services*, February 1991, pp. 67–77, 1991.

Hague G and Malos E, *Domestic Violence: Action for change*, New Clarion Press, 1993.

Haskey J, 'Lone parents and married parents with dependent children in Great Britain: a comparison of their occupation and social class profiles', *Population Trends*, 72, 1993.

Hester M, Humphries J, Pearson C, Qaiser K, Radford L and Woodfield K, 'Domestic violence and child contact'; in *Children Living with Domestic Violence* (Mullender A and Morley R, eds), Whiting and Birch, 1994.

Hill M, Lambert L and Triseliotis J, *Achieving Adoption with Love and Money*, National Children's Bureau, 1989.

Howe D, *Attachment Theory for Social Work Practice,* Macmillan, 1995.

Howe D and Hinings D, 'Adopted children referred to a child and family centre', *Adoption & Fostering*, 11:3, pp. 44–47, 1990.

Jewett C, *Helping Children Cope with Separation and Loss*, BAAF/Batsford, 1984.

Jordan V and Little W, 'Early comments on single parent adoptive homes', *Child Welfare*, 45, pp. 536–38, USA, 1966.

Kadushin A, *Adopting Older Children*, Columbia University Press, USA, 1970.

Kamerman S B and Kahn A J, 'What Europe does for single-parent families', *The Public Interest*, 93, 1988.

Kaniuk J, 'Openness in Adoption: Practice issues', *Exploring Openness in Adoption*. Adcock M, Kaniuk J and White R (eds), Significant Publications, 1993.

Kerrane A, Hunter A and Lane M, *Adopting Older and Handicapped Children*, Barnardo's Social Work Papers No. 14. Barnardo's, 1980.

Kirk H D, *Shared Fate: A theory of adoption and mental health*, The Free Press, USA, 1964.

Kirk H D and McDaniel S A, 'Adoption Policy in Great Britain and North America', *Journal of Social Policy*, 13:1, pp. 75–84, 1984.

Kitzinger C, *The Social Construction of Lesbianism*, Sage, 1987.

Kosonen M, 'Sibling relationships for children in the care system', *Adoption & Fostering*, 18:3, 1994.

Kumar V, *Poverty and Inequality in the UK: the Effects on Children*, National Children's Bureau, 1993.

Land H, 'The demise of the male breadwinner – in practice but not in theory', *Social Security and Social Change* (Baldwin S and Falkingham J eds), Harvester, 1994.

Lewis J, *Women and Social Policies in Europe: Work, family and the state*, Edward Elgar, ed 1993.

Logan J and Hughes B, 'The agenda for post-adoption services', *Adoption & Fostering*, 19:1, pp. 34–36, 1995.

Macaskill C, 'Post-adoption support: is it essential?', *Adoption & Fostering*, 9:1, pp. 45–49, 1985.

McGhee J, 'Consumers' views of a post-placement support project', *Adoption & Fostering*, 19:1, pp. 41–45, 1995.

McGuire J, 'Sons and daughters', Phoenix A, Woollett A and LLoyd E (eds): *Motherhood: Meanings, practices and ideologies*, Sage, 1991.

McWhinnie A, *Adopted Children: How they grow up*, Routledge & Kegan Paul, 1967.

Maluccio A N, Fein E and Olmstead K A, *Permanency Planning for Children; Concepts and methods*. Tavistock Publications, 1986.

Mason K, Hughes M and Selman P, *Adopting a Child with Down's Syndrome: Stage 3 of a Longitudinal Study*, Barnardo's, 1998.

Michaels G Y and Goldberg W A, *The Transition to Parenthood: Current theory and research*, Cambridge University Press, USA, eds 1988.

Middleton S, Ashworth K and Walker R, *Family Fortunes: Pressures on parents and children in the 1990s*, Child Poverty Action Group, 1995.

Miles M B and Huberman A M, *Qualitative Data Analysis*, 2nd Edition, Sage, 1994.

Millham S, Bullock R, Hosie K and Little M, *Lost in Care*, Gower, 1986.

Mullender A, *Open Adoption: The philosophy and the practice*, BAAF, 1991.

Murch M, Lowe N, Borkowski M, Copner R and Griew K, *Pathways to Adoption*, Research Report to the Department of Health, 1991.

O'Hara G, 'Developing post-placement services in Lothian', *Adoption & Fostering*, 10:4, pp. 38–42, 1986.

O'Shaughnessy T, *Adoption, Social Work and Social Theory*, Avebury, 1994.

Parker R, *Decision in Child Care*, Allen & Unwin, 1966.

Parker R, *Away from Home: A history of child care*, Barnardo's, 1990.

Parker R, Ward H, Jackson S, Aldgate J and Wedge P, *Looking After Children: Assessing Outcomes in Child Care,* The Report of an Independent Working Party established by the Department of Health, HMSO, eds 1991.

Phoenix A, Woollett A and Lloyd E, *Motherhood: Meanings, Practices and Ideologies*, Sage, eds 1991.

Rapoport R and R N, and Strelitz Z, *Fathers, Mothers and Others*, Routledge & Kegan Paul, London, 1977.

Raynor L, *The Adopted Child Comes of Age*, Allen & Unwin, 1980.

Rhodes P, *Racial Matching in Fostering*, Avebury, 1992.

Rhodes P, 'Charitable vocation or 'proper job'? The role of payment in foster care', *Adoption & Fostering*, 17:1, 1993.

Richards M, *Adoption*, Family Law in association with Jordan & Sons, 1989.

Richards M and Light P, *Children of Social Worlds*, Polity Press, Blackwell, eds 1986.

Rockel J and Ryburn M, *Adoption Today: Change and Choice in New Zealand*, Heinemann Reed, 1988.

Rowe J, *Yours by Choice: A Guide for Adoptive Parents*, Routledge & Kegan Paul, 1969 and 1982.

Rushton A, Treseder J and Quinton D, *New Parents for Older Children*, BAAF, 1988.

Rushton A, Treseder J and Quinton D, 'Sibling groups in permanent family placements', *Adoption & Fostering*, 13:4, pp. 5–11, 1989.

Rushton A, Quinton D and Treseder J, 'New parents for older children: support services during eight years of placement', *Adoption & Fostering*, 17:4, pp. 39–45, 1993.

Ruyek S, 'Feminist Visions of Health: An international perspective', in Mitchell T and Oakley A, *What is Feminism?*, Blackwell, 1986.

Ryburn M, *Open Adoption: Research, theory and practice*, Avebury, 1994.

Ryburn M, 'Adopted children's identity and information needs', *Children and Society*, 9:3, 1995.

Saradjian J, *Women who Sexually Abuse Children*, John Wiley & Sons, 1996.

Shireman J F, *Growing Up Adopted: An examination of some major issues*, Chicago Child Care Society, USA, 1988.

Shireman J F and Johnson P R, 'Single Persons as Adoptive Parents', *Social Service Review*, 50:1, pp.103-116, 1976.

Shireman J F and Johnson P R, 'Single-Parent Adoptions: A Longitudinal Study'; in the *Children and Youth Services Review*, 7, pp. 321–34, 1985.

Silverstein O and Rashbaum B, *The Courage to Raise Good Men*, Penguin, 1995.

Smith C R, *Adoption and Fostering: Why and how*, Macmillan, 1984.

Thoburn J, *Child Placement: Principles and practice* (2nd edn) Arena, 1994.

Thomas G V and Silk A M J, *An Introduction to the Psychology of Children's Drawings*, Harvester Wheatsheaf, 1990.

Thorpe M, Edwards R and Hanson A, *Culture and Processes of Adult Learning*, Routledge, 1993.

Tizard B, *Adoption: A second chance*, Open Books, 1977.

Tizard B and Phoenix A, *Black, White or Mixed Race?*, Routledge, 1993.

Trasler G, *In Place of Parents*, Routledge & Kegan Paul, 1960.

Triseliotis J, *In Search of Origins*, Routledge & Kegan Paul, 1973.

Triseliotis J, 'Some Moral and Practical Issues in Adoption Work', *Adoption & Fostering*, 13:2, pp. 21–27, 1989.

Triseliotis J and Russell J, *Hard to Place: The outcome of adoption and residential care*, Heinemann, 1984.

Triseliotis J, Sellick C and Short R, *Foster Care: Theory and practice*, BAAF/Batsford, 1995.

Ungerson C, *Gender and Caring*, Harvester Wheatsheaf, ed 1990.

Wallerstein J S and Kelly J B, *Surviving the Breakup: How children and parents cope with divorce*, Grant McIntyre, 1980.

Ward H, *Looking After Children: Research into Practice*, The Second Report to the Department of Health on Assessing Outcomes in Child Care, HMSO, ed 1995.

Watson L, *Developing post-placement support: A project in Scotland*, BAAF, 1995.

Wedge P and Mantle G, *Sibling Groups and Social Work*, Avebury, 1991.

Signposts in Adoption

Policy, Practice and Research issues
Edited by Malcolm Hill and Martin Shaw

Adoption policy and practice have altered dramatically over the last 20 years. The types of children needing adoptive families are quite different, compared to those of a generation ago, as are the experiences of adoptive families. What are the important changes and key trends? And what are the major issues and controversies that have preoccupied adoption workers?

This unique anthology brings together seminal papers published in BAAF's quarterly journal, *Adoption & Fostering*, which have contributed to shaping adoption practice in recent years. They cover principles and trends, processes and outcomes, openness in adoption, ethnic and cultural issues and post-adoption support.

Signposts in Adoption will be invaluable for practitioners, academics and students and will prove to be an enduring record of the main debates in the adoption field.

292PP   ISBN 1 873868 53 7   £12.95 + £2.00 P&P

Order a copy from **BAAF Publications, British Agencies for Adoption and Fostering, Skyline House, 200 Union Street, London SE1 0LX.**

Whatever Happened to Adam?

Stories of disabled people who were adopted or fostered
Hedi Argent

This remarkable book tells the stories of 20 young people with disabilities and the families who chose to care for them. All the children are now more than 20 years old and *Whatever happened to Adam?* delves into their fascinating histories. Family members, including the adopted people themselves, relive their experiences and share their recollections of what it was really like – the joy and the sadness, the successes and failures, the good times and the bad – with a touching openness and without glossing over the difficulties.

Poignant, inspiring and immensely readable, this book will serve as a powerful and timely reminder that adoption can be tremendously rewarding for disabled children and for their adoptive and foster families.

256 PAGES   ISBN 1 873868 56 1   £12.95 + £2.00 P&P

Order a copy from **BAAF Publications, British Agencies for Adoption and Fostering, Skyline House, 200 Union Street, London SE1 0LX**

Children Adopted from Care ▬▬

An examination of agency adoptions in England – 1996
Gilles Ivaldi

Children adopted from the public care system in England: What age were they when they started to be looked after? How long did they wait for adoption? Did they ever return home? How many moves did they have? Here is a unique study which presents an accurate picture of the pattern of local authority adoptions and raises important questions for policy makers, elected members, managers and practitioners.

The research reports on the first detailed analysis of the Department of Health's Children Looked After database. The information is revealing, and in some cases, shocking. It also provides a benchmark against which local authorities can evaluate the performance of their child placement practice as well as reflect on how to improve their services.

A4   60 PAGES   ISBN 1 873868 60 X   £11.95 + £1.50 P&P

⭕ Order a copy from **BAAF Publications, British Agencies for Adoption and Fostering, Skyline House, 200 Union Street, London SE1 0LX**

Exchanging Visions ▬▬

Papers on best practice in Europe for children separated from their birth parents

The plight of children and young people separated from their birth parents is a major challenge to the European community, both in terms of preventing family breakdown and in providing compensatory substitute care.
MIKE STEIN, PROFESSOR OF SOCIAL WORK, UNIVERSITY OF YORK

Exchanging Visions is a selection of papers from BAAF's first ever European conference which focused on how to achieve the best possible outcomes for all children separated from their birth families. Reflecting the rich variety of workshops on offer, topics include: social policy and the status of children in society; improving the quality of foster care; meeting the needs of minority ethnic children; turning legal principles into practice; and the reality of participation in decisions for children in the public care system.

Exchanging Visions is essential reading for policy makers, researchers, social work managers and practitioners and all those committed to the welfare of children in today's Europe.

A4 88 PAGES PAPERBACK   ISBN 1 873868 59 6   £10.95 + £1.50 P&P

⭕ Order a copy from **BAAF Publications, British Agencies for Adoption and Fostering, Skyline House, 200 Union Street, London SE1 0LX**

Making it Alone ▬▬▬

A study of the care experiences of young black people
Lynda Ince

I didn't understand the difference between colour. I thought there was no difference. I thought they were my mother and father... that I was white, but then as I grew older, I saw that I was definitely different and I became more conscious.
NATALIE

Placing two black children in a white suburb with a white family was wrong. They could have placed me anywhere with a black family.
DAVID

Young black people in the care system have often had to "make it alone" because they find themselves cut off from their family and their origins and without a sense of their own identity.

In this study Lynda Ince examines the personal experiences of ten young black people who had been on care orders. All of them had spent part of their lives in transracial placements, and most of them experienced problems with their racial identity and felt unprepared for the process of leaving care. Casualties of poor planning, many of the study sample suffered multiple moves during their time in care and none felt adequately prepared for independence when they become adults.

Placing the findings of this qualitative study within the context of childcare legislation and the literature about black children leaving care, the author identifies the key issues which affected the young people she interviewed. She examines the effects of being in care, the significance of "race" and culture in the care experience; transracial placements; the benefits of contact with the birth family; and identity needs. The study also offers valuable insights into the experiences, feelings and opinions of the young black people who had been in residential institutions, foster care or placed for adoption, vividly described in their own words.

Ince examines the policies of the two local authorities which placed these young people, and highlights the need for better planning with a focus on same-race placements and better preparation for young people leaving care.

Making it Alone will be of value to everyone involved in planning and making placements for black children and black children of mixed parentage.

The study points to the lack of black staff, black foster carers and adoptive parents; lack of appropriate training programmes; and lack of guidance for staff on same-race placements or on racism in relation to children in care.
COMMUNITY CARE

A4   94 PAGES   ISBN 1 873868 51 0   £10.95 + £1.50 P&P

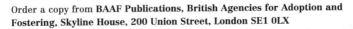

Order a copy from **BAAF Publications, British Agencies for Adoption and Fostering, Skyline House, 200 Union Street, London SE1 0LX**

adoption &fostering

**NEW DEVELOPMENTS IN
CHILDCARE PRACTICE AND RESEARCH**
QUARTERLY JOURNAL

*To my knowledge, the
journal is the richest
source of articles on
adoption and fostering
anywhere.*

JOHN TRISELIOTIS

*PROFESSOR AND
SENIOR RESEARCH FELLOW,
UNIVERSITY OF STRATHCLYDE*

Published four times a year by British Agencies for Adoption and
Fostering – a membership organisation – **adoption & fostering** is
at the forefront of debate on child care issues relevant to social
workers, social work managers, carers, medical practitioners,
lawyers, researchers and students of social work.

What the journal offers:

- a multidisciplinary approach to current debates
- contributors renowned in their fields both in the UK and overseas
- an international peer review panel
- a readable and authoritative voice
- medical and legal notes
- book reviews
- a review of research in practice

Keep abreast of the latest practice issues! Become a subscriber to
the UK's most authoritative journal focusing on adoption,
fostering and child care and you will receive four issues a year and
an index, with your subscription beginning in April 1999.

A free sample copy and subscription details are available from the
Production Editor, **adoption & fostering**, British Agencies for
Adoption and Fostering, Skyline House, 200 Union Street, London
SE1 0LX, UK. Tel 0171 593 2040 Fax 0171 593 2001.

British
Agencies
for **A**doption
and **F**ostering

Individual rate: UK **£37.50** overseas **£45.00**
Institutional rate: UK **£52.00** overseas **£65.00**
Student rate: (UK only) **£22.00**

80 PAGES   ISSN: 0308–9759